This book is due for return on or before the last date shown below.

A ... :ion

A PF
IN H

ROS

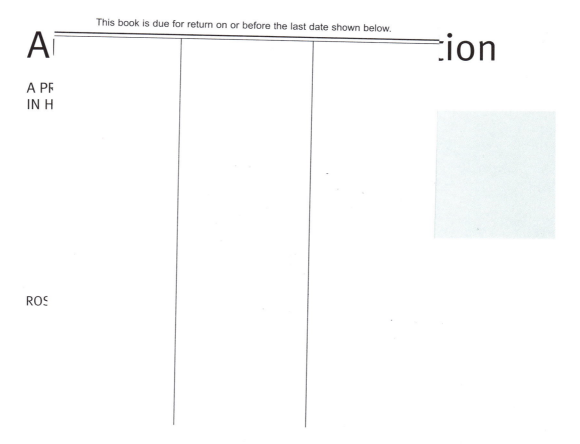

The King's Fund is an independent charitable foundation working for better health, especially in London. We carry out research, policy analysis and development activities, working on our own, in partnerships, and through grants. We are a major resource to people working in health, offering leadership and education courses; seminars and workshops; publications; information and library services; and conference and meeting facilities.

Published by:
King's Fund
11–13 Cavendish Square
London W1G 0AN
www.kingsfund.org.uk

© King's Fund 2003

Charity registration number: 207401

First published 2003

ISBN 1 85717 472 0

A CIP catalogue record for this book is available from the British Library

Available from:
King's Fund
11–13 Cavendish Square
London W1G 0AN
Tel: 020 7307 2591
Fax: 020 7307 2801
www.kingsfundbookshop.org.uk

Cover design by Minuche Mazumdar Farrar
Typeset by Grasshopper Design Company
Printed and bound in Great Britain

Outline

Part 1 considers why age discrimination has become a
topic on which increased attention is currently focused.
It acknowledges growing pressure from older people and
their organisations and it recognises the impact of the
National Service Framework for Older People and the
guidance on Fair Access to Care Services.

It continues with a look at how age discrimination
is defined and examines different kinds of age
discrimination including direct and indirect age
discrimination, ageism and ageist attitudes, and
age discrimination compounded by discrimination
relating to race, disability or gender.

Part 1 concludes by considering some common
concerns about the auditing process.

Awareness of and concern about age
discrimination has increased in recent years,
especially in health and social care bodies.
This has partly been in response to growing
pressure from older people and their
organisations. There have also been a number
of recent policy developments, including the
publication of a National Service Framework
for Older People and guidance on Fair Access
to Care Services. This section considers the
numerous factors that have placed age
discrimination higher on the agenda.

This section considers the difficulties in
defining and recognising age discrimination.
It looks at the many different forms of
discrimination, including direct and
indirect discrimination, ageist attitudes and
discrimination compounded by factors such as
race, disability and gender, and suggests that
multi-faceted approaches are needed to tackle
the issue. It concludes by describing some
common concerns about the auditing process.

Part 2   Gathering and assessing the evidence   17

Starting the process of auditing age discrimination in health and social care can be daunting. Part 2 offers guidance on gathering and assessing the evidence and suggests the use of an agreed framework as a basis for health and social care organisations to work together to combat age discrimination. It considers how age-related policies and practices can be assessed to consider their impact and whether or not they are fair.

Part 2 goes on to examine who should be involved in identifying age discrimination. It considers the role and composition of the scrutiny group and the crucial role of older people.

Age discrimination takes many forms, and Part 2 suggests areas for exploration where age discrimination may exist. It concludes by identifying and discussing some of the main sources of information and analysis about possible age discrimination.

Section 3 The audit framework   19

This section identifies common concerns in starting the process of auditing age discrimination in health and social care. It suggests the use of an agreed framework as a basis for health and social care organisations to work together in their area.

It then considers how age-related policies and practices can be assessed in order to make a judgement about their impact and whether or not they are fair.

Section 4 Who should be involved?   25

This section considers who should be involved in the process of identifying age discrimination. In particular, it examines the role and composition of the scrutiny group and how it can function most effectively.

The crucial role of older people in identifying age discrimination is then discussed and a range of ways of involving older people are reviewed.

need to develop strategies to address both explicit and implicit policies or actions that may result in age discrimination. This section gives examples of possible strategies and emphasises the importance of building on small actions that tackle discrimination towards larger and more effective efforts.

There are a number of key principles that help to make change happen in this area. This section sets out these principles and emphasises the importance of starting with small and achievable change, and working for continuing, incremental improvements within a strategic framework for change.

Contents

Foreword

The National Service Framework for Older People (NSFOP), published in January 2002, presented a major challenge for health and social care organisations to ensure they deliver fair, high-quality integrated services for older people. It is no coincidence that Standard 1 of the NSF is about rooting out age discrimination. This standard is the foundation stone of all the other standards since it acknowledges that tackling ageism and age discrimination remain important challenges for us all. If health and social care services for older people are – or are perceived to be – age discriminatory, they will not command the confidence of older people, nor of health and social care staff who deliver them. Ensuring that older people are treated according to their unique needs, circumstances and priorities will benefit not only older people, but all service users through promoting a culture of person-centred care.

Health and social care organisations need to be able to demonstrate that they are working to eradicate any age discrimination in access to services and quality of services. This is not as simple as it sounds, since age discrimination is more often subtle than it is blatant.

This guide, produced by the King's Fund, is very important in bringing together the experiences of those who have been working hard to identify age discrimination, as a first step towards eliminating it. It draws on early lessons and suggests a range of approaches for local action. It is particularly welcome that the guide focuses attention on the central role of older people in working with health and social care professionals to create the kinds of services they want and need, delivered in ways they prefer. It is also very helpful that the guide goes way beyond the formal identification of age discrimination in formal polices. The real challenge will indeed be to look at all areas of policy and everyday practice in order to genuinely root out ageism and age discrimination, and to develop modern and fair health and social care services with, and for, older people. The practical approach taken by the King's Fund will assist all those who are working together to achieve these goals.

Professor Ian Philp, National Director of Older People's Services

About the author

Ros Levenson is an independent policy consultant and researcher, and a visiting fellow at the King's Fund. She has written about a wide range of health and social care issues. Ros's early career was in social work and social services training. Her interest in health service issues and in user involvement developed during ten years as a community health council member and she later became Director of the Greater London Association of Community Health Councils for five years. Ros is currently a non-executive director of an NHS Trust, where she is a champion for older people and a member of the local scrutiny group on age discrimination.

Acknowledgements

I would like to acknowledge the many individuals and organisations whose ideas and experiences contributed to this guide. In particular, thanks are due to the scrutiny groups in Leeds, East Cambridgeshire and Fenland, and Brighton and Hove. Thanks also to Andy Barrick, Sara Corben, Carl Evans, Marylynn Fyvie-Gauld, Rita Garner, Tessa Harding, Pam Jones, Debra King, Susan LaBrooy, Pam Lloyd, Katrina McCormick, Lesley McDaniel, Barbara Meredith, Micky Wilmott, Mel Wright, Jane Yeomans and all the people who attended the King's Fund seminars in the summer of 2002.

Special thanks to Janice Robinson, who was a source of ideas and support throughout the whole process of working on the guide.

Ros Levenson

Introduction

About the guide

The purpose of this guide is to help all those who are involved in auditing age discrimination in health and social care. The guide is aimed primarily at people engaged in age discrimination scrutiny groups, as required by the National Service Framework for Older People (NSFOP) (Department of Health 2001a) and Fair Access to Care Services (FACS) (Department of Health 2002a). We hope that it will also be useful for older people's forums and bodies charged with monitoring performance and reviewing or inspecting health care services.

One of the major principles of identifying and tackling age discrimination is that older people must be at the centre of the work. Their knowledge and experience of using – or trying to use – health and social care services cannot be second guessed by anyone else. Working as equal partners alongside health and social care staff at all levels, older people can 'tell it like it is'. That is not to say that all older people are clamouring to sit on committees and working parties, though some are. As with all other age groups, that kind of participation will appeal to some but not to all. It is essential for health and social care organisations to engage with older people in order to find ways to enable the involvement of older people in different ways that suit their varied preferences, and to support them in making their voices heard.

Many older people will be interested to share their views and experiences, and to steer the direction of what health and social care organisations are auditing. One older person, speaking at a King's Fund seminar, lamented that scrutiny groups – the bodies charged with the responsibility for auditing age-related policies – were not necessarily considering what was important to her as an older person. She felt that it was necessary to look at policies, but it was equally important to consider how older people are treated as human beings, as well as looking critically at the gaps in services and whether local and national priorities correspond to the priorities of older people.

This guide draws on the experiences of health and social care staff, older people, policy makers, local campaigners and others who are, or have been, involved in looking at health and social care services for older people. It is an early attempt to draw together ideas and experiences, which will need to be reviewed and updated as work continues. The guide has been developed in consultation with the Department of Health, voluntary organisations, older people, professionals, managers and other relevant groups with an interest in health and social care for older people.

In order to develop this guide, we have drawn on the experiences to date of a number of local scrutiny groups that have audited age-related policies. In addition, a number of individual managers, clinicians, staff in key voluntary organisations and older people provided written information and engaged in discussions to share their experiences.

In the summer of 2002, the King's Fund held three seminars to discuss the following issues: identifying age discrimination in health and social care; involving older people in auditing age discrimination; and making change happen. These seminars provided a rich source of information as well as many of the ideas and quotations that have been used in this guide. Feedback from the participants also confirmed that many people felt isolated and uncertain about how to audit age discrimination in health and social care, and it was clear that those attending the seminars derived a great deal of support and inspiration from one another. We hope that, to some extent, this guide can continue to promote shared learning in order to take forward the enormously important task of auditing and tackling age discrimination in health and social care.

What is in the guide

The guide sets auditing age discrimination in health and social care in the context of recent policy developments. Recognising the absence of a single or simple definition of age discrimination in health and social care, Part 1 considers different forms of age discrimination, including direct and indirect age discrimination. It also assumes that effective audits of age discrimination must extend beyond a formal audit of policies, and must include informal and unwritten policies and practices. Indeed, the guide works from the premise that ageism in behaviours and attitudes, as well as in institutional practice, is at the heart of much age discrimination, and therefore it is essential to consider attitudes as well as policy. In Part 2, the guide looks at gathering and assessing the evidence of age discrimination, with particular reference to who should be involved, what to look at and where to look. Part 3 considers how to make change happen. It is clear from the interviews, observation visits and seminars that bringing about change to address age discrimination is widely seen as the hardest part of the process. Our message is clear: it is essential to start somewhere, even if it means beginning with small changes, as part of a larger strategic approach to change.

Age discrimination can exist in the provision of all types of services and in employment. The guide looks at how to develop audits of health and social care services, but it does not include in its scope any audits of employment policies or practices. Age discrimination in employment can affect the quality of services to older people as well as having direct implications for older people who are personally affected by age discrimination in the workplace. Our focus in this guide, however, is on age discrimination in relation to access to, and the appropriateness and quality of, health and social care services for older people. We hope that it will be a useful tool in the ever-increasing body of information and experience on identifying and ultimately rooting out age discrimination in health and social care.

How to use the guide

The guide is designed for use in different ways by different people. Those who lead on services for older people in health and social care organisations and those who are involved in auditing age discrimination may wish to read it in its entirety. Others may wish to refer to specific sections, for example on who should be involved in auditing age discrimination, or considering policies and beyond. There is a summary of each part and each section at the beginning of the guide to help you find the information you need easily.

Throughout the guide there are icons to assist you:

 indicates a case study

 indicates a checklist or key questions

 indicates a link to a website

 indicates contact details for further information

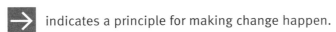 indicates a principle for making change happen.

Details of publications referenced within the text are included at the end of the guide and there is also a short section with details of useful websites.

Part 1
The policy context and definitions

Part 1 considers why age discrimination has become a topic on which increased attention is currently focused. It acknowledges growing pressure from older people and their organisations and it recognises the impact of the National Service Framework for Older People and the guidance on Fair Access to Care Services.

It continues with a look at how age discrimination is defined and examines different kinds of age discrimination including direct and indirect age discrimination, ageism and ageist attitudes, and age discrimination compounded by discrimination relating to race, disability or gender.

Part 1 concludes by considering some common concerns about the auditing process.

1 The policy context

Awareness of and concern about age discrimination has increased in recent years, especially in health and social care bodies. This has partly been in response to growing pressure from older people and their organisations. There have also been a number of recent policy developments, including the publication of a National Service Framework for Older People (NSFOP) and guidance on Fair Access to Care Services (FACS). This section considers the numerous factors that have placed age discrimination higher on the agenda.

Age discrimination in health and social care has been a concern of older people and their organisations for some years. This has focused on national age-related policies, such as age limits for breast screening. There has also been a great deal of concern in the last few years about charging for long-term care in England and Wales, which hits older people particularly hard as they are more likely than other age groups to need such care. In the social care context, standards set for accommodation for older people specify less room space per person than those for younger people.

There has also been concern about age discrimination at a local level. In health services, this has focused on whether older people are being denied access to particular treatments in some places, or whether they may be getting poorer access to services than younger people. Until recently, much of the concern about age discrimination came from older people and their organisations rather than from government or statutory health and social care bodies. Until the NSFOP, there had been relatively few systematic attempts to look for age discrimination or to address it if it was found.

What are the factors leading to greater scrutiny of age discrimination?

Official awareness of age discrimination in public services, including health and social care, has developed gradually and somewhat later than the awareness of discrimination relating to race, gender and disability. Unlike those other forms of discrimination, age discrimination is not yet the subject of anti-discrimination legislation in this country. However, this is set to change in the context of employment as the European Union Council of Ministers has adopted the Employment Directive on Equal Treatment (EU Council Directive 2000/78/EC), which requires all 15 European Union Member States to introduce legislation prohibiting direct and indirect discrimination at work on the grounds of age, sexual orientation, religion and belief and disability. The age discrimination legislation will be in place by 2006. A Department of Trade and Industry (DTI) consultation paper on getting the right framework to support equality legislation includes a section on age discrimination in employment (Department of Trade and Industry 2002).

There are a number of policy developments that have raised age discrimination higher on the agenda in recent years. Some of these are set out in Department of Health documents such as the *National Service Framework for Older People* (Department of Health 2001a) and *Fair Access to Care Services* (Department of Health 2002a). These are discussed below.

Work on ageism and discriminatory policies and practices has been given a huge impetus by the NSFOP, in which rooting out age discrimination is the first standard. It is also likely that a number of organisations have started serious work on rooting out age discrimination mainly because they are required to do so, rather than as a reflection of some prior commitment to doing so. In a number of cases discussed with people involved in scrutiny groups, a greater awareness of age discrimination, which has resulted from having to consider age-related policies, has formed the building blocks of a genuine commitment to eradicate age discrimination. More people in health and social care organisations now genuinely believe that modernised health and social care services, based around the needs of individuals and putting people at the centre of services, cannot be achieved if older people are not being listened to or treated fairly.

The impetus for rooting out age discrimination

While Department of Health guidance is a major driver in tackling age discrimination, the background factors that have lead to a growing concern about age discrimination in health and social care are more complex. A number of inter-related factors may be involved, as indicated in Figure 1 *opposite*.

The National Service Framework for Older People – Standard 1: Rooting out age discrimination

The NSFOP acknowledges that there has been discrimination against older people both in certain areas of health care and in social care. It states that denying access to services on the basis of age alone is unacceptable. Decisions about treatment and health care should be made on the basis of health needs and ability to benefit rather than a patient's age. In social care, assessed need should be matched to fair eligibility criteria for access to help and support (Department of Health 2002a).

Standard 1 of the NSFOP states:

> *NHS Services will be provided regardless of age, on the basis of clinical need alone. Social care services will not use age in their eligibility criteria or policies to restrict access to available services.*

Department of Health (2001a), p 16

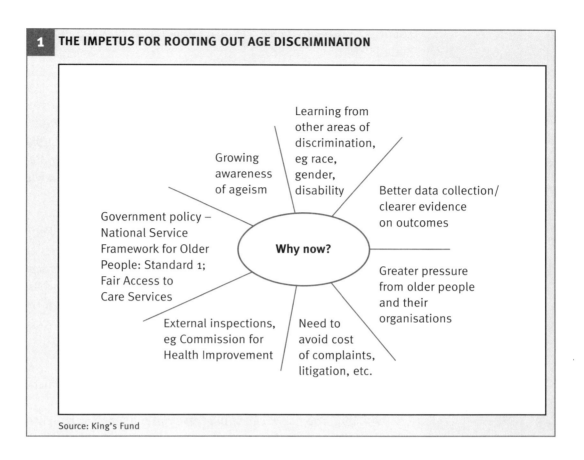

1 THE IMPETUS FOR ROOTING OUT AGE DISCRIMINATION

Learning from other areas of discrimination, eg race, gender, disability

Growing awareness of ageism

Better data collection/ clearer evidence on outcomes

Government policy – National Service Framework for Older People: Standard 1; Fair Access to Care Services

Why now?

Greater pressure from older people and their organisations

External inspections, eg Commission for Health Improvement

Need to avoid cost of complaints, litigation, etc.

Source: King's Fund

The NSFOP identifies a policy review checklist for the NHS as follows:

 ## A policy review checklist

- Identify all relevant policies and scrutinise for references to age, prioritising those areas where concerns have been raised.
- Set up a scrutiny group to review each policy, involving at least one non-executive director, representatives of patients and carers, clinicians and practitioners and managers.
- The scrutiny group reviews the reasons for each policy, including clinical evidence and patient and carer views.
- The scrutiny panel makes recommendations to the Board, which agrees a rolling programme of action.
- Details of the policy reviews, programme of action and results to be published in annual reports.

Fair Access to Care Services (FACS)

This guidance provides councils with a framework for setting their eligibility criteria for adult social care, and should be implemented by April 2003. It is intended that implementation will lead to a more consistent approach to eligibility and fairer access to care services across the country. At the heart of the guidance is the principle that councils should operate just one eligibility decision for all adults seeking social care support: that is, whether they are eligible for help or not. The guidance advises councils on work to tackle age discrimination as outlined in the NSFOP. Early guidance stated:

> *Through implementing this Fair Access guidance, councils will fulfil the first stage requirement of Standard 1 of the NSF for Older People with respect to rooting out age discrimination. Namely, they will achieve the milestone, originally set for April 2002, for reviewing their 'eligibility criteria for adult social care to ensure that they do not discriminate against older people'. Implementation will also assist councils to review wider policies for, and access to, adult social care in pursuit of Standard 1.*
>
> *The next milestone, for October 2002, in the NSF for Older People with respect to tackling age discrimination relates to the analysis of levels and patterns of services, particularly in the NHS. More detailed guidance will be issued in 2002. Councils are encouraged to engage in this process, through their local NSF for Older People implementation teams, and to apply it to their own services.*
>
> Department of Health (2002a), p 16

This was updated by Local Authority Circular LAC(2002)13, which said:

> *By 7 April 2003 councils should use the guidance to review and revise their eligibility criteria for social care, in consultation with local stakeholders including current service users, carers, NHS bodies and other appropriate local organisations. From April 2003 councils should apply eligibility criteria based on this guidance to all new requests for help. The care plans of all cases open on April 2003 should be reviewed, and individuals' needs re-assessed, by the beginning of April 2004. Further reviews should be planned for cases that remain open.*
>
> Department of Health (2002e), pp 1–2

2 What is age discrimination?

This section considers the difficulties in defining and recognising age discrimination. It looks at the many different forms of discrimination, including direct and indirect discrimination, ageist attitudes and discrimination compounded by factors such as race, disability and gender, and suggests that multi-faceted approaches are needed to tackle the issue. It concludes by describing some common concerns about the auditing process.

It can be surprisingly hard for those involved in auditing age discrimination to agree on a definition and to recognise age discrimination. In the absence of legislation, there is no single 'official' definition of age discrimination. The NSFOP defines age discrimination as:

> Action which adversely affects the older person because of their chrono-logical age alone. Discrimination can also mean positive discrimination, that is action taken to promote the best interests of the older person. But the term 'age discrimination' is generally used in the negative sense in this NSF.
>
> Department of Health (2001a), p 151

It is important for people working together at a local level, including older people, to work towards a shared understanding of what constitutes age discrimination. This understanding may develop in the course of looking at local policy and practice.

A number of definitions make links between ageism and age discrimination:

> Age discrimination is the practical manifestation of ageism, which is a form of prejudice like racism or sexism.
>
> Help the Aged (2002a)

> Ageism and ageist assumptions run throughout our services and society. They affect legislation, policy and practice and the attitudes that older people encounter day by day. Pervasive ageism erodes self esteem and undervalues the roles older people play in the lives of their families and communities. Ageism results in exclusion for older people and deprives the rest of society of the benefits its older members could bring. It needs to be challenged wherever it is found.
>
> Help the Aged (2000)

Audits of age discrimination should not be delayed while a perfect and inclusive definition is sought. Much can be done by considering services with a simple question in mind: would older people get a different service if they were younger, on account of their age? If the answer is yes, it is worth investigating what is happening, why it is happening and how any adverse effects can be addressed.

Different forms of age discrimination

In this guide, we are looking at ways of auditing age discrimination in its various forms, including:

- formal policies
- informal and unwritten policies and practices
- direct and indirect age discrimination
- behaviours and attitudes that may be perceived as ageist and/or age discriminatory.

It is not sufficient to take a box-ticking approach to rooting out age discrimination. Rooting out age discrimination, like rooting out any other form of discrimination, requires a multi-faceted approach that considers what happens in practice as well as what should happen according to official policy. Therefore, it involves a consideration of organisational culture, individual behaviour, leadership and management, and an awareness of age discrimination by individuals and teams. Success in rooting out age discrimination depends on a shared understanding of what may be discriminatory, why it is important to tackle it and how to take action to eradicate it.

Age discrimination can take several forms:

Direct age discrimination

This occurs when people are treated differently or denied access to services on the basis of chronological age. It is comparatively rare. Examples include:

- restricted access to specialist neurological nurse support which, in some areas, is funded for under-65s only
- policy that includes only under-65s in the remit of a liaison psychiatry service
- age-related criteria for access to day surgery, rather than assessing individuals' fitness and ability to benefit
- age-related criteria for specific services such as stroke services, rehabilitation, etc.
- age-related criteria for intensive care beds
- different cost-ceilings (amounts that can be spent) in local authorities for older people requiring social care
- charging policies.

Indirect age discrimination

This occurs when people are treated differently or denied access to services because of a factor other than chronological age, but where that factor may particularly affect older people or where older people may be disproportionately affected. Examples include:

- palliative care services if they accept only people with cancer, thereby excluding older people who may have other terminal conditions that are less likely to occur in younger people (for example heart failure)
- difficult physical access to buildings, or clinics held in places poorly served by transport: these factors can be detrimental to anyone, but older people may be more likely to be adversely affected
- lower referral rates for investigations or treatments for older people with similar health problems to younger people, in the absence of clear evidence to support a different approach
- early discharge without appropriate support services, which may particularly affect people living alone, as do many older people
- requiring people to attend the GP surgery to request repeat prescriptions, rather than accepting telephone requests: this may affect older people more than younger people
- eligibility criteria that effectively exclude many older people (*see* the case study *below*).

The older person is always discriminated against in hospitals – for example they get moved around more in hospital.

Occupational therapist, member of scrutiny group

 Case study: Indirect age discrimination

Over 90 per cent of the estimated one million registered or registrable blind or partially sighted people in the UK are over pensionable age. When asked about tasks they needed help with, the most commonly reported problem was cutting their toenails. Failure to get help with this can mean that people are unable to walk around and may suffer the usual consequences of poor foot care – both factors leading to wider problems relating to health, well-being and social participation.

However, in many areas podiatric services are being curtailed and restricted to those 'in clinical need' only. This effectively rules out visual impairment as a criterion for provision. Given that sight loss is so age-related this decision disproportionately impacts upon older people.

Source: Andy Barrick, Royal National Institute of the Blind (RNIB)

Ageist attitudes and hidden discrimination

Discrimination is underpinned by ageist attitudes that value older people less than younger people, or patronise them by denying their capacity to make choices. These attitudes can lead to policies and practices that discriminate against older people in subtle ways. Examples include:

■ addressing older people by first names or as 'dear' without ascertaining preferences
■ drawing a distinction between 'adults' and 'older people', as though older people were not adults
■ assuming that older people may not 'need' to be as fit as younger people who are in paid employment
■ stereotypical assumptions that older people are a homogenous group; failing to appreciate individuality and diversity
■ assuming that all older people are confused
■ ignoring the views of older people who have dementia or are confused
■ patronising older people, or excluding them from key discussions about their health and social care
■ variations in rates of treatments and social care facilities, even in the absence of age-related policies, and in the absence of evidence of need and ability to benefit from the intervention.

Multiple discrimination – age and race, age and disability, age and gender

Age discrimination may be compounded by other factors, and an older person may be doubly or triply discriminated against on account of age and race, age and disability or age and gender, or any combination of these and other factors.

In carrying out the audit and any subsequent action it will be important to take into account the views of older people from black and minority ethnic groups who may be particularly disadvantaged and may be likely to suffer more discrimination in accessing services. From April 2001 the Race Relations (Amendment) Act 2000 places a legal general duty on public bodies to promote equality and is backed by duties requiring consultation, monitoring and impact assessment of new policies on the promotion of race equality.

Similarly many older people in contact with health and social care services may as a consequence of disability be disadvantaged. The Disability Discrimination Act 1996 made it unlawful for service providers to refuse unjustifiably to provide a service to a disabled person available on similar terms to other people. Since October 1999 service providers have been under a duty to make reasonable adjustments to practices, policies or procedures which make it impossible or unreasonably difficult for disabled people to use a service.

Department of Health (2001b)

Case study: The inter-relationship between age and gender

A study in Yorkshire looked at different treatments and outcomes for men and women who had had a heart attack. Women were shown to be less likely to receive specialist treatment and life-saving drugs after a heart attack than men, and they tended to do less well afterwards. While this appeared be gender-related, it seems that, in fact, age was also a significant factor since the women who were studied were older than the men. The study concludes that under-treatment of older people may contribute to worse outcomes for women after acute myocardial infarction. It concludes that patients admitted to hospital with acute myocardial infarction should be offered optimal treatment irrespective of age or gender.

Source: Summarised from findings of Hanratty *et al* (2000)

It is important to make links with other work that may be taking place in health and social care organisations to address these different kinds of discrimination.

Some common concerns and worries

Auditing age discrimination is a fairly new concept for most health and social care organisations. At the outset, different people involved in the process may have a range of concerns about the process itself or about the implications of identifying areas where discrimination will need to be addressed. These fears may be explicit or implicit, but it is important to recognise them as they can impede the audit if they are not taken seriously. These are some of the concerns that may inhibit scrutiny of age-related criteria at a local level:

- Discriminatory practices will require huge resources if they are to be addressed.
- There is a shortage of evidence on what is appropriate and effective health care for older people.
- The quality of data is low, and this makes it difficult to know what is happening at a local level.
- Clinicians may not admit to ageist attitudes and behaviours, and they may believe that they are basing their decisions on clinical need.
- There may be attention to service areas where age discrimination is measurable, rather than those areas where it is equally significant but harder to quantify. This may lead to undue emphasis on certain service areas such as surgical procedures.
- There may be concerns about the relevance of evidence in a health and social care system in which organisation, treatment and care are constantly changing.
- Tackling custom and practice demands a huge change agenda.

It is useful to encourage the members of a scrutiny group to discuss their concerns and worries about auditing for age discrimination. They can then consider whether their concerns are based on fact, and how they can be addressed.

Part 2
Gathering and assessing the evidence

→

Starting the process of auditing age discrimination in health and social care can be daunting. Part 2 offers guidance on gathering and assessing the evidence and suggests the use of an agreed framework as a basis for health and social care organisations to work together to combat age discrimination. It considers how age-related policies and practices can be assessed to consider their impact and whether or not they are fair.

Part 2 goes on to examine who should be involved in identifying age discrimination. It considers the role and composition of the scrutiny group and the crucial role of older people.

Age discrimination takes many forms, and Part 2 suggests areas for exploring where age discrimination may exist. It concludes by identifying and discussing some of the main sources of information and analysis about possible age discrimination.

3 The audit framework

This section identifies common concerns in starting the process of auditing age discrimination in health and social care. It suggests the use of an agreed framework as a basis for health and social care organisations to work together in their area.

It then considers how age-related policies and practices can be assessed in order to make a judgement about their impact and whether or not they are fair.

We are looking at issues, not just discrimination. You can't easily get people to talk about discrimination, but we say: tell us what your issues are.

Non-executive director, PCT

We know age discrimination is there but older people don't recognise it and tend to go along with it.

Member of a scrutiny group

Identifying age discrimination in health and social care settings

It can be difficult to identify discrimination in health and social care settings for a number of reasons:

FACTORS THAT MAKE IT DIFFICULT TO IDENTIFY AGE DISCRIMINATION

- Not everyone is familiar with the concept of age discrimination so it is not always recognised.
- Comparatively few policies are overtly age discriminatory – most age discrimination is subtle.
- There is comparatively little research on the outcomes of some treatments for older people; it can be difficult to know whether a decision to treat or not to treat an older person in a particular way is evidence-based.
- Health and social care professionals may not be aware of their own ageism.
- Older people themselves may be ageist and some may accept discrimination as the norm or expect to be treated differently because of their age.
- Seeking information about age-discriminatory policies and practices is a new and relatively under-developed area.
- It is not always obvious whether shortcomings in health care and social services are related to age discrimination or whether they need to be addressed across all age groups.

A framework for an age discrimination audit

Audits of age discrimination should be planned and carried out using an agreed framework so that all health and social care agencies in the area can proceed from a shared understanding of what they are looking at and how to take action, where necessary, to address and ultimately eliminate age discrimination.

In devising a framework, there is much to be learned from experience in assessing the impact of other forms of discrimination. One example can be found in the following case study.

 Case study: Devising a framework for Leeds

Leeds West Primary Care Trust (PCT) leads the action on age discrimination scrutiny for Leeds as a whole. Early experience showed that all the local PCTs, acute hospitals and mental health trusts approached the age discrimination audit in different ways and with differing degrees of thoroughness. The scrutiny group looked at the audits and acknowledged the need for a standardised tool. This led to the development of a Framework for Age Discrimination Audit. This was based on the Race Equality Impact Audit Guidance Manual, produced in July 2001 by the Equal Opportunities Unit at Leeds City Council.

In the Leeds Framework for Age Discrimination Audit, the auditing and action planning process involves the completion of three forms:

The Audit Planner Form is designed to assist with the planning and co-ordination of the audits. The form is to be completed by the Older People's contact for the organisation. That person is asked to identify the organisation's or department's functions and a lead person within each service who will be asked to complete the audit and action plan form.

The Audit Form is designed to assist services to identify elements within each service that may discriminate against older people. This should be completed by the lead person for each service, identified from the audit planning process.

The Action Plan Form. Services are asked to produce an action plan taking into account the issues identified through the auditing process. This is to be completed by the lead person for each service. The Older People's contact will then amalgamate the service action plans into a single organisational/departmental plan, which is presented to the scrutiny group and boards.

When agreeing a framework for auditing age discrimination, it is important to consider the following key questions:

 Key questions for agreeing a framework for auditing age discrimination

- Do you have an agreed framework for your age discrimination audit?
- Do all health and social care organisations know what it is?
- Does it draw on lessons learned from audits of other kinds of discrimination?
- Does it look at the impact of age discrimination on services and service users?
- Does it include a way of identifying multiple causes of discrimination (for example race, disability, gender)?
- Is it reviewed to ensure that it remains relevant?
- Does it identify lead people and a clear process?
- Does it link in to the NSF Local Implementation Team?
- Does it link in to wider decision and policy making processes?
- Does it link in to an action planning process?

How to judge whether policies and practices are fair

Judging whether policies and practices are fair will not always be straightforward:

> *It is important, but not always easy, to differentiate between areas where elders are treated differently, or receive a different kind of service, simply because of their age – which would strongly indicate policies or practices which, whatever the intention, are discriminatory in their effect; and differences which are the result of differences in need, complexity, or the pattern of demand for service – which may be entirely justifiable.*

London Borough of Tower Hamlets (2001)

Effective scrutiny of age-related policy and practice may well bring to light examples of:

- policies and practices that are detrimental or discriminatory to older people (for example age-related barriers to accessing services)
- policies and practices that are not age-related, but which may impact differentially on older people (for example long waits for therapies and other interventions may be more significant to older people in some circumstances)
- policies and practices that are age-related and where prevailing professional opinion believes these are required to enable a needs-related service to be delivered (for example sessions for over-75 health checks, flu jabs)
- policies and practices where age-related differences reflect user and/or carer preferences or special needs (for example support for older people who are involved on committees and groups in health and social care organisations)
- policies and practices that positively discriminate in favour of older people (for example podiatry services for older people).

A key question is: how can you tell if age-related policies and practices are justifiable? It is important to take stock of all age-related policies and practices, and all policies and practices that may impact differently on different age groups. You may hear a variety of possible justifications, or there may be no apparent reason other than long-standing custom and practice. You will need to think critically about whether justifications that are offered for age-related criteria are acceptable in the context of modern health and social care services. The checklist opposite is designed to help you do so. Further discussion of some of the arguments put forward in defence of age-related policies are critically examined in a King's Fund paper (Robinson 2002).

In some areas of practice, there are divided opinions, or uncertainty, on the appropriateness – or otherwise – of age-related services. One of the main areas where this debate continues is about how acute medical care for older people should be organised in hospitals. The checklist can be applied to this issue, but opinions may vary, especially on questions 2, 3 and 4. One geriatrician's view is set out below:

> *Current concerns about age discrimination and the Department of Health's recent reviews of age discriminatory policies have highlighted an issue which concerns not just older people but the public as a whole – equity of access to specialist medical and surgical services. Should everyone with an illness related to one organ, such as the heart or the stomach, have access to a specialist in that field? Can some conditions be treated by all doctors? If older people are frail and have multiple problems, should geriatricians be in charge of their care? Will that deny them access to other specialist care? Can these decisions be made by virtue of age alone? Do wards for older people provide more benefit by concentrating multi-professional and multi-disciplinary care or are they perceived as places where the care that is offered is second-rate?*
>
> *Many older members of the public perceive that admission to geriatric wards or services excludes them from appropriate specialist care, and if they are otherwise fit and well they may feel that it does not best serve their needs.*
>
> *Although separate geriatric care has often pioneered effective and holistic care for older people, it is perhaps time to review how we could best serve the spectrum of needs for the diverse group we call 'older people'. This may mean that we have to be clearer about what kinds of treatment and care are best offered by geriatricians and the multi-disciplinary team that they work with, and what is best offered by other specialties, calling on the geriatrician for particular expertise when necessary.*
>
> Dr Susan LaBrooy, consultant geriatrician

Different but equal or different but worse? Making a judgement on whether age-related criteria are fair and justifiable

The National Service Framework for Older People (NSFOP) is clear that age discrimination must be rooted out. But how can you tell whether age-related criteria in relation to health and social care for older people are discriminatory, or whether they are fair and consistent with meeting older people's needs and preferences, or can be justified on any other grounds? Here are some questions to help you make that judgement:

Question 1 Do age-related criteria in relation to specific health or social care services allow for some flexibility to reflect the needs of individuals?
Examples of this might include enabling younger people with dementia to use specialist services that may be used most often by older people, or enabling an older person with learning disabilities to use services that primarily serve younger people, provided that the services continue to be appropriate for the individual.
YES/NO

If the answer to this question is no, it is likely that the age-related approach cannot be justified in all cases. Given that older people are very different from one another, and some people in their nineties can be fitter than some people in their fifties, it is essential that age-related criteria must have some flexibility, even if they can usually be justified as the best way to meet the needs of older people.

Question 2 Is there research evidence to support the effectiveness of an age-related model of service delivery?
If so, what is the evidence and is it robust? Does it include research findings that are based on older people's experiences, for example were older people included in clinical trials on effectiveness of medicines?
YES/NO

If the answer to this question and its subsidiary questions is no, age-related criteria may not be justified.

Question 3 Is there evidence of older people preferring an age-related model of service delivery?
Examples of this might be special wards, day centres or other services used exclusively for older people.

If so, what is the evidence and is it robust? Does it allow for different preferences among older people? Is the evidence reasonably recent in order to reflect changing views and values?
YES/NO

If the answer to this question and its subsidiary questions is no, age-related criteria may not be justified.

Question 4 Are age-related criteria justifiable by organisational factors?
Examples of this might be specialist services for older people with similar needs or the need to have a critical number of people in order to offer specialist services, or to ensure an appropriate skill mix in the staff group.
YES/NO

If the answer to this question is no, age-related criteria may not be justified.

Question 5 Do older people benefit from age-related criteria?
Examples of this might be positive discrimination for access to podiatry or rapid access to physiotherapy.

If so, is there evidence of greater effectiveness as a result of age-related criteria? Can these age-related criteria be implemented without causing unacceptable/adverse clinical or social consequences to other age groups in relation to their needs?
YES/NO

If the answer to this question and its subsidiary questions is no, age-related criteria may not be justified.

Question 6 Are age-related criteria justified mainly or solely on the grounds of saving money?
YES/NO

If the answer to this question is yes, age-related criteria are unjustified.

Question 7 Are different age groups assumed to have different expectations of a quality of life that facilitates independence and social participation?
YES/NO

If the answer to this question is yes, age-related criteria are unjustified.

Question 8 Are age-related criteria justified by value judgements that older people have had their life, or that their lives are less socially or economically valuable than those of younger people?
YES/NO

If the answer to this question is yes, age-related criteria are unjustified.

Who should be involved?

This section considers who should be involved in the process of identifying age discrimination. In particular, it examines the role and composition of the scrutiny group, and how it can function most effectively.

The crucial role of older people in identifying age discrimination is then discussed and a range of ways of involving older people are reviewed.

Scrutiny groups

The scrutiny group will comprise only a small proportion of those who should be involved in effective audits of age discrimination. Each health and social care organisation or department will need to develop a mechanism and a lead person for ensuring that where age discrimination exists, it is reported to the scrutiny group. The scrutiny group may itself need to be supported by a wider reference group in order to facilitate effective communication with staff in health and social care organisations, and with older people and the wider community (*see* Figure 2 *below*).

What is a scrutiny group?

The first mention of scrutiny groups was in the National Service Framework for Older People (NSFOP). No specific date was given by which they were to be set up, but the task that they were given – to review policies for reference to age – was to be

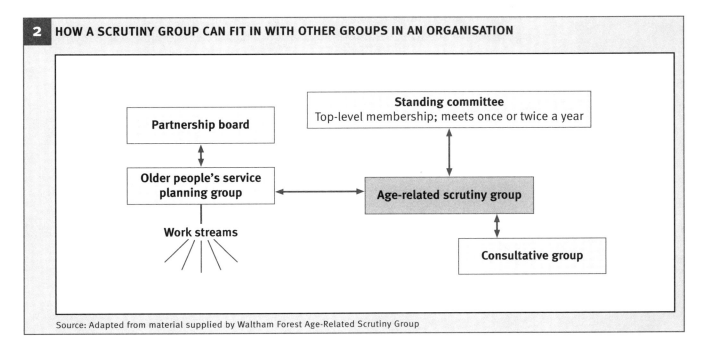

2 HOW A SCRUTINY GROUP CAN FIT IN WITH OTHER GROUPS IN AN ORGANISATION

Source: Adapted from material supplied by Waltham Forest Age-Related Scrutiny Group

completed by October 2001. The configuration of scrutiny groups has varied across the country, reflecting local organisational structures. Their function has been to oversee a systematic approach to identifying and eliminating age discrimination in health and social care.

Who should be in the scrutiny group?

The Department of Health stated that establishing a scrutiny group was the responsibility of the Chief Executive Officer (CEO) with overall responsibility for the NSFOP, in liaison with the Local Implementation Team. These groups have generally been functioning for some time, with the suggested core membership of:

- a non-executive champion for older people
- a council champion for older people
- clinical practitioner/champion(s) for older people
- user group representative(s), including older people
- carer representative(s)
- a project manager identified by the Local Implementation Team and agreed by all CEOs in the local system to ensure that the manager has ready access to information in all organisations.

In practice, scrutiny groups seem to be working in very different ways. The checklist below highlights some questions that you can ask to see how well your scrutiny group is working.

 ## Scrutiny group health check

Work programme
- Is the group clear as to its purpose?
- Does the group have a clear programme of work, with identified leads and timetables?
- Is there a programme to address explicit polices, unthinking or insensitive provision of services, staff awareness, attitudes and behaviour, and unwritten policies, custom and practice?
- Is the work programme reviewed at regular intervals?

Who attends?
- Has the group secured core members as indicated by the Department of Health?
- Are all relevant local health and social care organisations involved?
- Do they attend regularly?
- Are the people from health and social care organisations of sufficient seniority to be effective on the group?
- How has the scrutiny group addressed the possibility of tokenistic participation of older people and carers, and ensured that it moves beyond tokenism?

When and where does it meet?

- How frequently does the group meet?
- How do you assess whether this frequency is satisfactory?
- Is the time of day suitable for all members, including older people and carers?
- Is the venue accessible for all, including older people and carers?
- Is the venue seen as neutral and acceptable to all members?

Support

- Does the scrutiny group have adequate administrative support?
- Do individual members of the scrutiny group receive support, as required, in order to maximise their effective participation in the group?
- Is training and development available to members of the scrutiny group, to reflect their common and different needs?
- Are older people reimbursed for their out-of-pocket expenses, including travel and carer costs (if required)?

Taking action

- Has the scrutiny group reported in the annual reports of local health and social care organisations?
- Has the scrutiny group identified mechanisms for translating analysis into action? (see pp 55–63)
- Is the scrutiny group aware of action that is planned or has been taken to root out age discrimination, and any barriers to doing so?

Involving older people

It's the tea and bingo syndrome. We want to contribute. We may have bad knees and legs, but we have meaningful contributions to make.

Older person, speaking at King's Fund seminar

Your needs change as you get older. When you were younger, you'd have had no idea what you would want.

Older person, speaking at King's Fund seminar

@
See:
www.bettergovernment
forolderpeople.gov.uk

Involving older people is at the heart of effective auditing of age discrimination. There is a wealth of experience to draw on in relation to user involvement in general (Barker *et al* 1999; Cabinet Office 1999a, 1999b; Better Government for Older People website) and about involving older people specifically (Herklots 2002; Ellis *et al* 2003). However, most efforts to involve older people have focused on seeking views on service developments or on the quality of services. While many of the principles of good practice from those areas apply to the scrutiny of policy and practice and to the identification of discrimination, there may also be some refinements that are more specific to this new area of work.

There are a number of good-practice principles that need taking into account to ensure that older people are involved in auditing age discrimination (*see* the checklist *below*).

 Effective involvement of older people: some general principles

- The involvement of older people in audits of age discrimination should be part of a strategy on patient and public involvement.
- Think about who you want to involve and why you want to involve them, and be explicit about this.
- Be clear about whether you are involving people for their personal experiences and opinions or whether you are looking for them to build links with a wider group of older people and/or have a representative function.
- Be aware of the diversity of 'older people': the needs and views of a 60-year-old may be quite different from those of a person of 95; race, gender, disability, area of residence, etc. may all be relevant.
- Avoid tokenism – do not expect one person to 'represent' the diversity of older people's views.
- Attend to practicalities such as suitable venues, transport and payment of expenses.
- Don't look for a single method to involve all older people.
- Go out to older people – don't expect them always to come to you.
- Involving older people should be part of an ongoing dialogue, not a one-off approach.
- Offer background information and support to maximise the participation of older people.
- Communicate effectively what has happened as a result of the involvement of older people.
- Identify resources to support the involvement of older people – it may not be very expensive, but some money and staff time will be required.

Effective ways of involving older people in identifying age discrimination

There is no blueprint for what works, and certainly no single one-size-fits-all approach that will work everywhere and for everyone. Local circumstances, the existence of local groups and networks, whether the population is urban or rural, the enthusiasm of individuals – these and many other factors can influence success or limit it in practice. However, there are valuable lessons to be inferred from other contexts in which older people have been involved in (or excluded from) influencing health and social care. There is also a growing body of expertise from specific attempts to involve older people in auditing age discrimination. Some of these approaches are described below.

Direct involvement of older people on scrutiny groups

Older people and carers are important members of scrutiny groups, and there are many instances of older people being effective and valued members of such groups. However, it can be difficult for any lay people, whatever their age, to function effectively when they may feel different from the health and social care professionals and managers who make up the greatest number on the group. It is likely that some support will be needed to facilitate effective involvement, and some financial resources should be allocated for this purpose.

Some scrutiny groups have found ways of supporting older people on scrutiny groups by:

- **Pre-meeting briefings**: to explain the background to agenda items and answer questions that older people may wish to clarify in advance of the meeting. These briefing meetings can be held immediately before the full scrutiny group meets in order to make the best use of time
- **Jargon-busting**: while avoidance of jargon is good practice, it is not always observed. One scrutiny group has devised a system of 'yellow cards' that people can hold up when jargon is used by others in a way that is inappropriate or incomprehensible. This can be a non-threatening way to bring the problem to light. The yellow card system can be operated in a spirit of fun, while being genuinely useful for those who tend to use jargon as well as those who are on the receiving end of it
- **Ensuring that several older people are present at the scrutiny group**: isolation and a feeling of tokenism can be very off-putting to older people. Ensuring that several older people are invited to attend can encourage the contribution of each individual
- **Ensuring that the group members get to know one another**: many members of the group will already have professional working relationships. Older people on the group may not know all the other participants, and need a chance to do so.

 Case study: Training for older people auditing age discrimination

In South East London, when the NSFOP was published, an Older People's Multi-Agency Liaison Group (OPMAG) was set up to take forward the NSFOP across Lambeth, Southwark and Lewisham (LSL). Membership of OPMAG included representatives from the three borough social services departments, the primary care organisations, the mental health trust and the acute trusts. OPMAG decided that the audit of policies for age-related criteria would best be done across LSL. OPMAG was mandated to act as the local scrutiny group, with additional membership to include non-executive directors, local authority councillors, and service users and carers.

When older people and carers were invited to take part in the local scrutiny group, the initial letter inviting nominations stated:

> *To support the involvement of older people, carers and patient representatives we will be holding a facilitated half-day seminar to inform people of how the review will take place and seek their views on how they can best be involved. Refreshments, travel expenses and respite care expenses will be provided. The time commitment will be attendance at the half-day workshop and two, two-hour meetings. The person would also need to be willing to contribute their views in a group setting and to represent others' views as well as their own.*

The workshop was attended by 12 people; lunch was provided and a £10 gift voucher was given to all attendees. The views expressed at the workshop were written up and presented as a report to the scrutiny group. Two people from the group subsequently agreed to attend the local scrutiny group on behalf of older people and carers.

When the LSL-wide OPMAG disbanded it was replaced by borough-based scrutiny groups. In Lewisham this took the form of a 'whole system' scrutiny group, comprising health and social care organisations across the borough, plus the non-executive directors and local authority councillors. From the beginning this group stated: 'Training and support will be provided to lay representatives to enable full participation in the scrutiny group.'

A training event was held in October 2002 as part of this commitment to prepare for the first borough-based scrutiny group.

Katrina McCormick, public health specialist, says: 'Scrutiny for age discrimination in health and social care services is a new function. Offering support to older people and carers in terms of a "facilitated training event" has provided an opportunity for them to explore and describe their views on age discrimination.'

> *i*
> For further information, contact Katrina McCormick.
> Email:
> Katrina.McCormick @lewishampct.nhs.uk

The limits of direct questioning about age discrimination

One general lesson that seems to be emerging is that direct questions about age discrimination are not always very successful in obtaining answers, though useful information has been obtained through national surveys (Age Concern England 1999). Older people often have no way of knowing if their experiences reflect age discrimination. They do, however, know what it is like to try to obtain services and they know what it was like to use those services if they obtained them. Older people often have many constructive ideas on how the quality of their services can be improved. Tuning into these ideas may be a better way of getting insights into age discrimination than relying on direct questions in isolation from a broader discussion about access and quality. It will then be for the scrutiny group and for supporting staff in health and social care organisations to consider which aspects of the issues raised by older people are best understood and addressed within the context of age discrimination, and which issues are best dealt with in other forums that address service standards. Either way, the information obtained from older people will not be wasted, provided that there are adequate links between the scrutiny group and other appropriate structures.

Locally administered questionnaires

Opinion is divided on whether local questionnaires on age discrimination are an effective way to involve older people in audits of age discrimination. Most experience to date suggests that the effort involved is rarely justified by the quality or quantity of the information received. Some of the limitations of the questionnaire approach to seeking information about age discrimination follow:

- Low response rates are common, particularly for postal questionnaires.
- Formulating suitable questions is very difficult – how do older people know whether they have experienced age discrimination or poor services for some other reason?
- Questionnaires cannot usually address subtle aspects of an older person's experience of health and social care in order to enable an assessment of whether age discrimination is a significant factor.
- Questionnaires are not usually able to capture qualitative data as effectively as some other methods.

As a result of trying a questionnaire-based approach, the East Cambridgeshire and Fenland scrutiny group took the view that a more personal approach – going out to meet older people – was much more productive.

Reference groups and advisory panels

Although a scrutiny group may seek to include a range of people, it will remain a fairly small group. Other ways need to be found to seek the views and expertise of a wider group of older people. A wider reference group or advisory panel can enable the participation of a larger number of older people and can enable the participation of some who might find regular committee attendance a burden. In this way, age discrimination and other related quality issues can be addressed more comprehensively. It will often be possible to invite an existing group or forum to act as a reference group or advisory group, thus lessening the need for too many meetings. In any case, it may be helpful to consider the possibility of a time-limited involvement for individuals on scrutiny groups and reference groups. This may encourage some people to become involved. It may also bring in different views and expand the number of people involved.

Ongoing dialogue

One-off discussions about age discrimination are of very limited value. Better communication and more useful information may emerge from opportunities for ongoing dialogue involving older people. This can and should extend to a much wider range of older people than can reasonably be involved in a scrutiny group. This can take many forms. Most areas already have useful mechanisms for dialogue, and these should be used wherever possible, rather than setting up unnecessary additional bureaucratic structures. Local opportunities for dialogue may include older people's forums (*see* the box *overleaf*) or other standing groups. As patients' forums come into existence and develop, they should also be able to play a full part in local dialogue as well as promoting local involvement.

Unless we get regular, respectful dialogue, it tends to be set pieces.

PCT public health lead

OLDER PEOPLE'S FORUMS

Older people's forums are the voice of older people in their own locality. They first came into being in 1990 and are now widespread throughout the country. Since 1998 the Better Government for Older People (BGOP) programme has encouraged the direct involvement of older people in developing policy and services.

Forums are run by and for older people. Their role is to represent the views of older people on local matters and take up issues that are of concern to them. Forums are independent of statutory bodies and of any specific groups. They are concerned to make themselves as representative as possible of older people. Usually this will include links with groups of minority ethnic older people and older people with disabilities.

Older people are involved in many area Local Implementation Teams for the NSFOP, including scrutiny groups and other groups that are considering Standard 1 of the NSFOP on age discrimination.

See Help the Aged (2002b)

The following case study is an example of a local project to involve older people.

 ## Case study: Kilburn Older Voices Exchange (KOVE)

By October 2002, KOVE had been meeting for six months as a community panel consisting of older people in the Kilburn area and local service providers including resource centre, social work team, district nurse and community centre representation. The project has been funded and supported by Kilburn Single Regeneration and Camden Gold (a consortium of resource centre providers in Camden).

The aim of the project is to give a voice to older people in the area over current service delivery, changes in practice, forward planning and ideas for new initiatives. It is hoped that KOVE will help encourage organisations to involve older people in decision-making, and listen to their experiences and their ideas for improving services.

During this first phase of KOVE it has addressed a number of issues and also linked up with other groups of older people in the local community. Initially, some scepticism was expressed over service changes and promises. Comments from older people included 'nobody seems to listen' and 'they all tell me a different thing'.

However, positive comments were also made, including: 'That's good ... Let's do it together.'

KOVE involvement has included the following areas:

- **home care services**: raising issues of quality standards and promoting the involvement of older people in the induction and training of professional carers
- **accessible transport**: lobbying for more flexible transport with support for people with disabilities in order to offer people opportunities to socialise and have a better quality of life
- **quality of services**: challenging the quality of services when they do not provide what they say they should
- **advocacy and support of older people**: by supporting the development of independent information and advice services in the area and creating an accessible voice through KOVE for older people to express their views and needs
- **promoting independence**: spreading the word locally about health and social care services, and ensuring that older people understand what the services mean for them
- **primary care trusts**: understanding the changes in health services and reminding managers about the Camden PCT mission statement of listening to patients
- **podiatry services**: taking up specific issues of local services and working together with service managers to try and develop services with and for older people
- **access to and in local supermarkets**: publishing a KOVE fact sheet that informs people with disabilities what assistance is available for them to do their own shopping
- **common health conditions**: spreading the word about conditions such as diabetes that can be better managed when people develop their understanding of the condition.

i

For further information, contact Mel Wright, KOVE facilitator, c/o Lesley Rowe, Manager, Kingsgate Centre, 208b Webheath, Palmerston Road, NW6 2JU.

KOVE has developed ground rules for meetings, which include having a 'no jargon zone'. Professionals attending have to explain what they mean in clear language. Transport is provided for members who need it, and meetings take place in a warm and comfortable venue at a pace that is meaningful and as appropriate as possible for all present. Everyone is encouraged to contribute and meeting notes are produced so that each member is clear about what has been done and what is planned.

In October 2002, KOVE finished the first phase of its work. As current members were keen to continue, its future was under active consideration.

There are many other examples of ongoing panels and forums that involve older people in decision-making and in influencing health and social care organisations. Some of these, such as the Fife User Panels (Age Concern Scotland 1994; Barnes and Bennett 1998) particularly aim to involve older people who are unable to leave their homes without assistance.

Going out to people

Going out to places where older people meet or live may be a valuable starting point for getting dialogue going. Support workers in supported housing may be useful contacts initially. Social clubs and community groups may also be pleased to be involved in discussions with health and social care organisations.

> *Questionnaires had a low response. Then we blitzed the media, newsletters, parish councils, etc. – all to nil effect. So now I'm visiting all the places where older people are, eg, clubs, homes.*

PCT non-executive director

Telephone conferencing (teleconferencing)

Teleconferencing – bringing people together for a telephone discussion – offers a cost-effective and practical option for involving older people. It may be a particularly appropriate method of involving older people who are unable to leave their homes. For example, in Age Concern Waltham Forest (ACWF) teleconferencing has taken place since 2000, following a pilot project in 1998. It mainly involves older people from a waiting list of people needing volunteer visitors. ACWF has funding to cover this project and there is no cost to the client.

> **i**
>
> For further information, contact Lesley McDaniel, ACWF Link-up Project Co-ordinator. Email: lesmack @canfieldroad.fsnet. co.uk

The ACWF teleconferencing session normally involves five or six older people and an Age Concern facilitator. The group talks for half an hour a week for eight weeks. Health and social care are popular subjects for discussion. The older participants are keen to have an opportunity to make known their views on age discrimination and the quality of health and social care services to those who are responsible for them. The facilitator observes:

> *The groups are eloquent on their views but often feel helpless because of their disabilities, and all are concerned that people see them as a nuisance.*

> **i**
>
> For further information, contact Community Network.
> Tel: 020 7923 5250.
> Website: www. community-network.org
> Email: Terry@ community-network.org

Teleconferencing can be arranged through Community Network, a registered charity based in Islington. The majority of referrals are by word of mouth. Each half-hour call involving five or six people costs between £15 and £17 including VAT. This is not a premium rate service and normal call charges apply. No equipment is needed apart from a normal telephone.

> **i**
>
> For further information, contact Andy Barrick, Assistant Director, RNIB Information and Advocacy Services, 105 Judd Street, London WC1H 9NE.
> Tel: 020 7391 2230

Another organisation that has used teleconferencing is the Royal National Institute of the Blind (RNIB). RNIB has launched a telephone conference facility that brings together groups of people over the telephone to discuss their needs, views and experiences in a focus group. Discussions are taped and this enables RNIB to involve people who would otherwise be unable to participate in traditional consultation exercises. It also offers the possibility of running groups in different languages and supporting patient self management. There are clear possibilities for learning from RNIB's experiences in adapting teleconferencing to obtain people's views on age discrimination, and using this method to illustrate people's needs and experiences in a very direct way to staff and managers in health and social care organisations.

Listening events/consultations

While one-off events have their limitations, they can be valuable. They are most likely to be useful where they have a clearly defined focus, for example listening to older people from black and minority ethnic communities, or listening to views on a particular range of services. All the usual rules of effective consultation apply, such as ensuring good planning, providing a suitable venue and assistance with transport, setting up effective publicity and providing honest feedback on actions resulting from the meeting.

Advocacy

While most older people are perfectly capable of representing their own views, there are circumstances in which advocates can assist and empower them to do so. Older people with dementia, older people whose first language is not English and those with health-related communication difficulties (for example after a stroke) may benefit from access to advocacy support in making their views known. The purposes of advocacy with older people in hospital have been described in a report from the Older People's Advocacy Alliance (OPAAL) UK (Dunning 2000). Advocacy is more often used to empower individuals to use services effectively. It is less well developed as a means of enabling older people to make their views and opinions known in a wider context, and there is much scope for development here, provided that older people are enabled and empowered to speak for themselves whenever possible.

5 What to look at – policies and beyond

Age discrimination in health and social care takes many forms. This section suggests areas where it may be productive to look for possible examples of age discrimination. This includes: policies; custom and practice; access to specific services; attitudes; privacy and dignity; the environment; information and staffing.

Policies and beyond – the need for a broad approach

It is important to look at policies, but it is also important to consider some of the other ways in which age discrimination can manifest itself. Policies do not give the whole picture, but scrutinising them can be a good way in to a broader examination of what is really happening. It is also important to consider subtler forms of age discrimination. This may include the exclusion of residents of residential and nursing home care from some aspects of primary care, misdiagnosis of older people's mental health problems, long waits in accident and emergency departments, negative attitudes, inappropriate hospital discharge arrangements, and inadequate arrangements for rehabilitation and long-term support.

Health policies

While it is essential to look systematically at the whole range of policies, it is necessary to distinguish between national and local ones. For example, age criteria for breast screening derive from national policy, which is justified by reference to evidence of effectiveness and the benefits to those who are screened. The evidence base on which it draws is changing and is disputed by some, and is now being reviewed.

When looking at local policies, it is also useful to be aware of where discrimination has been identified elsewhere. Areas of policy and practice where age discrimination has commonly been identified include: upper age limits for a range of hospital services and operations; age-related policies on admission to high dependency units; explicit age barriers in admission to cardiac care units and cardiac rehabilitation; rationing of community health services on the basis of age; exclusion of older people from clinical trials; age-related differences in access to colonoscopy, thrombolysis and interocular surgery; age-related criteria for admission to day surgery units and admission to care of elderly and rehabilitation wards; and age-related criteria for access to liaison psychiatry (Roberts 2000; Roberts *et al* 2002; Help the Aged 2002a). In the NHS, a number of written policies with age-related criteria were identified by audits and reported to the Department of Health (*see* Table 1 *opposite*).

TABLE 1: WRITTEN POLICIES WITHIN THE NHS WITH AGE-RELATED CRITERIA IDENTIFIED IN AUDITS BY SERVICE AREA*

PRIMARY CARE	SECONDARY CARE	COMMUNITY CARE	MENTAL HEALTH
Management of coronary heart disease	Resuscitation	Podiatry (P)	Mental health (service organisation)
Hypertension	Hospital admission policies	Continuing care	Liaison psychiatry
Chiropody (P)	Access to day surgery	Community rehabilitation teams	Rehabilitation
Audiology (P)	Emergency admissions	Older people's support teams (P)	Clinical psychology
Gastroentorology screening		Physical disabilities teams	Alcohol dependency services
Osteoporosis screening		Community neuro rehabilitation units	
Over-75 health check (P)	Older People – specialist teams	Health visiting	
Flu vaccination (P)		Community dietetics	
Breast screening		Integrated living teams	
Cervical cancer screening		Therapy (P)	
	Adverse clinical incident reporting	District nursing (P)	
	Pressure sore management (P)	Referral to palliative care	
	Transplant policy	Stroke care (rehab)	
Prescribing		Pressure sore management (P)	
Colorectal cancer screening			
	Anaesthesia guidelines		
	Coronary heart disease clinical guidelines		
	Neurology		
	Immediate stroke care		

* This table excludes areas such as IVF and child-related services, which are considered irrelevant in this context.
(P) = examples of positive discrimination by age

Source: Adapted from Department of Health (2002b) p 5

It is also important to have a mechanism for scrutinising new policies and emerging practices to ensure that they do not discriminate against older people. For example, many areas now have specialist general practitioners. Older people may benefit from these specialist services along with all other age groups. However, while specialist GPs are supposed to enhance access to specialist services close to home, some older people fear that they will not be able to get patient transport services to take them to primary care and community clinics, so they may end up less able to access services than before. Therefore, scrutiny of policy needs to look at both strategic and operational aspects and the key question in this context is: what does the policy mean in practice to people of all ages?

Health (organisations) either said we don't have discriminatory policies, or else they squirreled policies away or said 'which policies do you want to see?' Social services are driven by policies and protocols, but health didn't know what we are talking about.

Head of Partnership Working in a PCT/member of a scrutiny group

Social care policies

In social care, the most common policy area with age-related criteria is the existence of a different cost ceiling for packages of care. In the past it has been common practice for there to be a policy that sets limits to the cost of packages of care for older people at a lower level than for younger people, regardless of individual needs. Another discriminatory practice is exemplified by having a system of automatic review when any package of care reaches a 'trigger level' of cost. At that point, the package of care is reviewed to see whether or not other forms of care may just as appropriately meet the service user's needs in a more cost-effective way. In practice, the cost of residential care has been used as the trigger for review. If this is applied across the board, it is not necessarily discriminatory, but in practice older people are seen as a single group with similar needs, while younger people's needs are assessed on a case by case basis. Also, the average costs of residential care for older people are less than the costs of residential care for younger disabled people. Therefore older people reach the trigger level for review, and experience probable pressure to accept residential care, more readily than do younger people.

Some local authorities have decided to look at policy, practice, guidance and institutional ageism in a systematic way. This has shown areas of concern that may not be obvious from a narrower focus on written policies. For example, the following areas may become evident:

- Problems of transition between services triggered by chronological age rather than changing needs. For example, people with learning disabilities may be required to transfer from the specialist learning disabilities service to a generic older people's service once they reach the age of 65, regardless of individual need and personal circumstances. Older people with mental health problems may be required to transfer to the care of the psychogeriatric service (in health care organisations) or the older people's team (in social care organisations) regardless of individual needs.
- A focus on maintenance rather than development and empowerment in patterns of service for older people. An example of this might be where major effort was put into enabling younger disabled people to be involved in community activities or consultations, in contrast with simply providing services for older people.
- A greater tendency for older people to be without a named care manager once services are in place, in comparison with younger people.
- In some areas, better access to bathing for younger people (who have personal care provided according to need) than for older people able to have a weekly bath only through a bathing service.
- Different levels of staffing and training for staff in services for different age groups.

The following case study considers an audit of age discrimination in social care.

Case study: Age discrimination in social care

The Royal Borough of Kensington and Chelsea (RBKC) undertook a thorough initial audit on age discrimination. A small steering group was formed, comprising commissioners/purchasers, and planning and development personnel and practitioners, and used information gathered from the Better Government for Older People Group and the Older Person's Health and Social Care Reference Group.

The audit, which took place in 2001–2, looked at policy, practice, guidance and institutional ageism in the following areas:

- care homes
- meals services
- home care
- occupational therapy (OT)
- transport
- finance
- general
- funding of voluntary organisations
- day care.

Each section considered:

- the age discriminatory issues
- the effects of age discrimination
- what could be done by RBKC (which might also mean cross-divisional action)
- what action could be taken outside the remit of RBKC.

It was recognised that some actions would be beyond the remit of the audit group and the local authority, but it was felt that it would be beneficial to draw attention to ageist practice, which is often underpinned by attitudes that extend across boundaries.

> **i**
> For further information, contact Pam Jones. Email: pam.jones @rbkc.gov.uk

Custom and practice

Most age discrimination is not enshrined in formal policies, but is the result of custom and practice that has developed over time. In so far as this may reflect underlying ageist assumptions, it may lead to disadvantaging older people. It is hard to identify discrimination in everyday practice precisely because ways of working have become embedded. Usual procedures are seen as the right or inevitable way of doing things, given pressures on staff time. These are the areas where it is often most difficult to bring about change.

To give just one illustration, no hospital would ever have a policy that deliberately discriminated against older people in terms of proper nutrition. However, some custom and practice may have exactly that effect. For example, some older people cannot open sandwich packets, and there may be no-one available to help them do so. This very small aspect of daily practice may discriminate against older people. It is also an illustration of how identifying very small changes with few cost implications may have a large effect on the experience of older people in health and social care.

Seeing the service through the users' eyes and listening to what they say is the best way of uncovering custom and practice that discriminates against older people. It is also an essential perspective when seeking remedies to the problem.

Access to specific services

> *You get to 70 and you begin to see what you are not eligible for and how you are treated. For example, I was told not to worry about cholesterol past 65, but I spoke to a doctor from the USA and he said 'What! Of course you should.' Older people are not always given statins [medicines to help lower cholesterol].*
>
> Older person, speaking at a scrutiny group

As we have seen, access to some services has historically been restricted on age criteria as a result of explicit policies, but that is comparatively rare. It is much more common to find that access is restricted because of either a failure to realise that older people might benefit from a service (see case study below), or because the service is organised in such a way as to deter older people from wanting to use it.

 Case study: Older people and alcohol services

In the initial reports to the Department of Health on audits of age-related policies, relatively few instances were reported of restricted access to alcohol services for older people. However, according to the Alcohol Concern Directory of Alcohol Services (2000/01) there were at least 23 health authorities operating an upper age limit for alcohol services. It seems that this kind of age discrimination can be invisible when local audits are carried out.

Age Concern Wandsworth's conference report is available at: www.aclondon.org.uk/findaboutacs/acil-activities.htm

Wandsworth Age Concern has been active on this issue and has had a project and a conference on older people and alcohol misuse. It was found that access and provision of suitable and appropriate alcohol services for older people was undermined by a presumption that this is not a service for older people. However, anecdotal data from frontline staff working with older people, as well as local older people and their carers, highlighted a number of alcohol-related concerns among people over the age of 60. In the project's experience this situation is not exclusive to Wandsworth but is far more pervasive.

There has been little research nationally on alcohol and older people and this lack has contributed to the development of services and interventions that do not reflect the needs of an older population. Despite numerous generic studies highlighting links between alcohol misuse and rates of depression and morbidity, older people remain an often excluded and isolated population.

For professionals working with older people the consequence is often that alcohol use is not appropriately assessed or recorded. The division of specialist teams working with elderly people often mean that there is very little alcohol awareness or relevant training to support staff, and this adds to the effect of alcohol-related harm being mismanaged between teams.

The Age Concern Wandsworth project is working on the following key areas:

- working with teams for elderly people to assist in the development of appropriate care packages for older people with alcohol problems
- developing protocols for joint working between alcohol and elderly services
- raising awareness among professionals and teams working with older people of alcohol misuse and services for people with alcohol problems
- supporting alcohol misuse agencies in developing the ability of their services to meet the specific needs of older people
- providing specialist training events, bringing together alcohol and elderly services, on effective provision for older people with alcohol misuse problems.

There are many other areas that may or may not have formal barriers to access, but where the nature of the service may be a deterrent. Health education and health promotion frequently lack a focus on older people. Older people are rarely targeted for smoking cessation, even though there may be no formal barriers to access; the presumption appears to be that younger people will be the main users of the service. Safe sex campaigns are usually focused on the young, with a stereotypical assumption that older people will not need to be targeted. Underlying this is a notion that older people only need 'older people's services', when in fact they may need access to many of the services that are needed by all other age groups.

Attitudes

The most frequently reported aspect of age discrimination is the prevalence of ageist attitudes. Audits of age discrimination can be a useful vehicle for staff and older people to work together to look at current practice and work towards more respectful and empowering attitudes. The box *overleaf* lists some of the more common ageist attitudes.

AGEIST ATTITUDES AND ASSUMPTIONS

- Assuming that all older people are similar in their needs, regardless of their health, social circumstances, age, race, gender, disability and personal values and preferences.
- Assuming that older people are unable to participate in decisions about their own treatment and care, usually because of assumptions about their capacity to understand.
- Assuming that older people are less valuable members of society than people of working age.
- Assuming that older people will not want/need to be in peak health.
- Assuming that health problems are 'just your age'.
- Assuming that older people are less interested in preventive measures to safeguard their health.
- Assuming that older people will (or will not) want specific treatments or services, without asking them.

Privacy and dignity

While privacy and dignity are important issues for all people, older people in health and social care are particularly vulnerable to breaches in good standards due to the greater level of dependence that older people may have when they are ill or in need of care. Audits of possible age discrimination should involve older people, carers and health and social care staff in identifying areas of concern. These may include:

- audibility of consultations and discussion of personal matters
- lack of proper cubicles or screens around treatment areas
- lack of care in maintaining appropriate clothing
- lack of privacy in bathrooms and toilets
- inappropriate discussion, without the permission of the older person, with relatives and carers.

Help the Aged led a campaign on dignity on the ward and a number of publications are available (Dunning 2000; Help the Aged 1999a; Help the Aged 1999b; Help the Aged 2001).

Environment

The physical environments within which older people are treated and cared for should also be the subject of attention to ensure that age discrimination does not result in older people having a poorer environment for their health and social care than younger people. This may sometimes seem a daunting area to consider, as the solutions can be very costly. However, some of the issues requiring attention may be quite small. Those that are larger and require capital investment also need to be identified so that appropriate planning can take place for future investment and improvement.

The use of mixed-sex wards is recognised to be particularly distressing for older people. Although this issue is being addressed nationally, local work can ensure that appropriate developments are taking place in a timely manner.

The following checklist considers questions to ask about the environment in which older people receive health and social care services.

 Key questions about the environment

- How do wards, clinics and facilities in which older people are commonly treated compare with other facilities?
- If there is a department of medicine for older people, is it located in suitable premises, and are standards comparable with other facilities in the hospital?
- Are there sufficient suitable bathing and toilet facilities to meet the needs of older people?
- Are mixed-sex wards being adapted for single-sex use as quickly as possible?
- Are facilities for rehabilitation adequate and conveniently located?
- Are public telephones in health and social care buildings suitable for older people, including those with hearing or visual impairments?
- Is the environment safe for older people (for example, is there suitable flooring to minimise the risk of falls)?
- Do large-scale improvements for older people's facilities in health and social care requiring capital investment get fair shares when prioritising decisions are taken?

Information

Barriers to do with use of professional language and jargon which excludes users is in our power, and indeed is our responsibility to change. It is easy to slip into jargon, but we should challenge ourselves, and each other when this happens . . . There is no reason to take the view that issues will be too complex for older people to understand, and it is patronising and ageist to suggest that this is the case.

Herklots (2002), pp 30–31

While information about health and social care for all people may be less than perfect, older people may be disadvantaged by ageist attitudes that deny them access to the best possible information. Both oral and written information are important to enable older people to make informed choices and decisions about their own treatment and care. Inappropriate assumptions are sometimes made about the level and nature of information that older people require, and older people are sometimes assumed to want less information than younger people, though there is no evidence to support this.

The quality of written information is clearly of major importance to all, and clear type fonts in a large enough size to be read easily, with good contrast may be particularly valuable to older people. It is also important to review what kinds of information are provided and to ascertain whether there are gaps in information provision. For example, while many information leaflets are available on specific conditions and treatments, are older people fully informed about what rehabilitation may consist of after a fall or a stroke?

Local reviews to assess the information needs of older people are required as part of the action plans within the Department of Health's Information Strategy for Older People in England (Department of Health 2002c).

Staffing

It is important to see whether staff caring for older people in health and social care are as well trained as those caring for younger people. It is also important to consider staff ratios and skill mix in relation to needs.

Findings

- An early audit in the Royal Borough of Kensington and Chelsea's social services department found that, in comparison with younger people with physical disabilities and mental health problems, a higher proportion of older people were not assessed or reviewed by qualified care managers.
- Research at the Sussex Rehabilitation Centre, reported to the Brighton and Hove scrutiny group, indicated that the nursing pay budget per bed was £22,827 for beds on a ward for people under 65 and £20,913 for those on the ward for people over 65. Although the needs of the older age group were generally greater, the pay budget per bed was eight per cent lower for the nurses caring for the older age group.

These examples have been chosen because they are likely to be replicated elsewhere; there is no suggestion that these audit findings are exceptional.

Where to look – sources of information and evidence about age discrimination

There are so many sources of possible information about age discrimination that it can be hard to know where to start. In addition to analysing written policies, many other areas of practice will need to be examined. Each of these may draw on a different permutation of sources of qualitative and quantitative information and evidence. This section identifies and discusses some of the main sources to consider for information and analysis about possible age discrimination.

In addition to a Specialist Registrar looking at paper policies, there has been inclusion of the voluntary sector and there has been work with the older people's forum. However, most older people do not report any perception or experience of discrimination as such. Enquiries have to be subtler, for example discussion about how they view services generally. Older people are often inhibited by their experience of ageism; for example they feel they are seen as 'bed blockers'. Older people also need dialogue and reassurance about changes to health care practices (for example cataracts under local anaesthetics).

Discussion at Leeds scrutiny group

Department of Health benchmarking tool

Available at:
www.doh.gov.uk/nsf/
olderpeople.htm

In November 2002 the Department of Health issued a first version of a tool designed to help those responsible for commissioning or delivering services at a local level to compare patterns of treatment at different ages with those in other areas. The tool is provided as a computer-based model available as a Microsoft Excel file and is available from the NSFOP website. There is also a helpful User Guide to accompany the tool, which includes notes on accessing and interpreting the data and some worked-through examples to illustrate the kinds of information that are available and questions that can be raised by an analysis of the data.

The tool displays comparative information on treatment rates at different ages, and on the balance between treatment rates for different age groups. It contains data from the Hospital Episode Statistics (HES) for 2000–2001 on ten acute hospital procedures:

- elective* coronary artery bypass grafting (CABG)
- elective* percutaneous transluminal coronary angioplasty (PTCA)
- elective* cardiac valve procedures

* Note: While the vast majority of admissions for these selected procedures will be elective, the figures do not exclude emergencies or those for which the admission type is unknown.

- elective* cardiac pacemaker implantation
- elective* hip replacements
- elective* knee replacements
- elective* cataract procedures
- elective* hernia procedures
- varicose vein procedures
- breast cancer surgery.

These procedures were selected for a number of reasons. They represent treatments frequently performed on older people, although not exclusively so. They relate to conditions where some concerns have been expressed about adequacy of access in old age. They comprise procedures that can have a considerable impact on quality and/or length of life.

For each procedure, background data contains intervention rates per 10,000 resident population by health authority (HA) and strategic health authority (StHA). Some procedures are shown with rates for seven different age bands. Others, however, are shown with rates for just four different age bands. This is because the numbers of these procedures performed on people aged 85 and over are so low that it would not be reliable to compare local rates for these procedures by narrow age bands.

As there is no simple, generally agreed, appropriate rate for each procedure at each age, data about intervention rates are not enough to draw conclusions about possible age discrimination. Therefore, the tool also provides information about the ratios of procedure rates between older and younger people. These ratios are the key variables to be benchmarked. Where data have allowed, four different ratios have been calculated:

- **general old to young ratio**: the over-65 intervention rate divided by the under-65 intervention rate
- **ratio of mature to old and very old**: the rate for those aged between 65 and 74 divided by the rate for those aged 75 and above
- **ratio of mature and old to very old**: the rate for those aged between 65 and 84 divided by the rate for those aged 85 and above
- **ratio of old to very old**: the rate for those aged between 75 and 84 divided by the rate for those aged 85 and above.

The benchmarking tool allows comparison of data for a selected HA or StHA with:

- all HAs in England
- all StHAs in England
- HAs in the same StHA
- HAs in the same ex-regional office
- HAs in the same Office of National Statistics (ONS) cluster – grouped on the basis of a number of socio-economic variables
- a user-defined group of authorities.

* Note: While the vast majority of admissions for these selected procedures will be elective, the figures do not exclude emergencies or those for which the admission type is unknown.

In addition to rates and ratios of treatments by age group, the tool includes the facility to take account of a number of factors that may be helpful in considering whether local variations can be explained by factors not associated with age discrimination:

- average length of stay and average waiting time by procedure, age band and health authority of residence (HES data 2000/01)
- life expectancy at birth (years) by sex and health authority of residence (UK figures 1998–2000, ONS 2000)
- healthy life expectancy at birth (defined in terms of expected years of life in self-reported good or fairly good health), by health authority (1992–98 figures for England, ONS 2002).

In sum, the Department of Health's initial benchmarking tool is a useful starting point for local health and social care staff, voluntary organisations and older people to take stock of age-related variations for a number of acute elective procedures. At a local level, the key questions may include:

- Is the local situation broadly in line with comparable areas?
- If not, what factors might explain those variations?
- Are there indications of age discrimination and, if so, for which age groups and for which interventions?
- How can action be taken to root out inappropriate age-related variations in treatment ratios?

WHAT THE DEPARTMENT OF HEALTH TOOL CAN DO

- It provides robust data on intervention rates for a number of elective, acute procedures.
- It provides some context in order to make comparisons more appropriate.
- It can be analysed to make comparisons with other authorities or groups of authorities.
- It can be used to focus attention at a local level on age-related variations in relation to these specific procedures.
- It can and should stimulate critical analysis of local variations to ascertain whether these suggest age discrimination, specific local needs or other factors.

WHAT THE DEPARTMENT OF HEALTH TOOL CANNOT DO

- It cannot provide information on what the intervention rates or ratios *should* be for any particular age group in any particular area.
- It cannot provide answers to why variations in age-related treatment ratios exist – it is a useful starting point towards asking the right questions in order to get answers.
- It cannot provide data relating directly to primary care trust (PCT) or local implementation team (LIT) boundaries or councils. Scrutiny groups and other interested parties will need to liaise and work closely with their StHA and other LITs in the area to obtain full benefit from using the tool.
- It cannot yet provide information on primary care and social care interventions. It is anticipated that subsequent updates of the tool will also include data on age-specific interventions in primary and social care settings.

Other statistical information on local services

Many health organisations have had the benefit of input from a public health consultant or specialist registrar in identifying age discrimination. This is extremely helpful in getting to grips with sometimes complex statistical data. A public health perspective can be helpful in analysing current practice and suggested changes to services. For example, bed numbers can be difficult to understand, and changes in numbers and bed usage may sometimes conceal changes that particularly impact on older people. For example, a postal survey of lead clinicians in geriatric medicine in English NHS Trusts conducted by the British Geriatrics Society (BGS) during December 2001 and January 2002 found that 21 per cent of respondents reported that mainstream hospital beds – mainly rehabilitation beds – had been switched to intermediate care use, in some cases with a reduction in the total number of beds available. Also often cited was the redesignation of community hospital beds and proposals for GP-led and nurse-led intermediate care beds. Concern was expressed regarding responsibilities for such beds and the lack of medical input for nurse-led intermediate care beds (Age Concern and British Geriatrics Society 2002).

External reports

Some information on reported or apparent age discrimination may be available from reports made on health and social care organisations by a range of bodies including the Commission for Health Improvement (CHI), the Social Services Inspectorate (SSI), the Intensive Support Team (part of the Modernisation Agency), or past reports from Community Health Councils (to be abolished in 2003) or those from voluntary organisations. In some cases, these reports will relate to a specific NHS or social care body, and will give direct pointers to areas of concern. In other instances, CHI reports and other reports in the public domain that have been written about other organisations may indicate areas of age discrimination to which attention could also usefully be drawn in your own organisation.

Information about the performance of hospitals (star ratings), published annually by the Department of Health, and information about the performance ratings of PCTs, published for the first time in 2002, may also be used to compare local and national performance and provide clues on areas to examine in terms of age discrimination.

Statistical data and figures on beds and other services are important sources of information, but they will need to be carefully interrogated in order to understand the implications for older people.

Research

Locally commissioned research can be very helpful in looking at services for older people and finding out whether they are actually being discriminated against in practice. Research projects need not be elaborate or large. They may be undertaken in-house or in collaboration with university departments.

Two accounts of research into age discrimination are given in the following case studies.

Case study: Basic needs interviews

Semi-structured interviews were conducted with patients on two wards (one for patients under 65 and one for patients over 65) in Sussex Rehabilitation Centre, Shoreham, Sussex, which is part of South Downs Health Trust. The interviews sought to investigate how people's basic needs were met on the ward. Each interview focused on three areas:

- **bathing and washing arrangements**: frequency on the ward and at home, the assistance provided, preferences for the gender of the assistant and level of privacy afforded
- **food and eating arrangements**: general opinion of the food, the choice available, the menu arrangements, accessing the dining areas, the speed at which food was brought and satisfaction with assistance provided with eating
- **visiting arrangements**: how easy it was to maintain relationships on the ward in terms of space and time available for visitors, level of privacy and staff attitudes to visitors.

In each area, interviewees were asked for any general comments in addition to these specific questions. Interviewees were also invited to comment on any aspect of their care at the end of the interview. Each interview lasted between 30 and 50 minutes and interviewees were selected on the advice of nursing staff on each ward. This selection method was adopted to ensure that patients interviewed were able to understand the purpose of the interview and give informed consent.

The research elicited a wealth of qualitative material and also highlighted these specific findings:

- Patients on the wards for people aged over 65 received one bath every two weeks. In contrast, those on the ward for people under 65 received over two baths a week. This difference could only partly be explained by patient dependency ratings. It was suggested that the older patients were less likely to be concerned with bathing when a full wash is offered every morning. More in-depth interviews would confirm or refute this view.
- Waiting times for assistance varied across the two wards. The average waiting time on the ward for older patients was 10 minutes, compared with 4.2 minutes on the other ward. This difference could only partially be explained by patient dependency ratings.
- Nevertheless, there was no difference in satisfaction with the assistance provided by staff.
- There was a higher level of satisfaction with visiting arrangements on the ward for over-65s than on the ward for under-65s.

For further information, contact Rita Garner. Email: Rita.Garner @southdowns.nhs.uk

The findings indicated that staffing levels on the ward for older people were not sufficient. Given the higher levels of dependency on that ward, more staff would be required to bring service provision up to the standard of the ward for younger people. Although this research provided a snapshot and raised many questions as well as answers, it offered valuable insight into some age-related differences in care.

Case study: Research project in social care and mental health

The Health and Social Policy Research Centre at Brighton University was commissioned by Brighton and Hove PCT and South Downs NHS Trust to carry out a research project focusing on the attitudes of service providers towards older people. It was conducted as a part-time project over a four-month period, starting in Autumn 2002. The research took the form of a number of interviews with clinicians, other professionals and older people in receipt of care and non-participant observation. Interviews with older people took place in a variety of settings including day centres, hospitals and carers' groups.

The project's main aim was to evaluate the impact of age discrimination, first on the assessment of needs of people over 60 in receipt of social and mental health care, and second on their access to services. As a result of the research, examples of good practice will be highlighted and disseminated and recommendations made for improving policy and practice where appropriate.

Early findings suggest that discrimination can be seen in the lack of residential care especially for elderly mentally ill people. Elderly mentally ill people tend to be very dependent and have high levels of need. Low levels of need are, by their nature, cheaper to provide and since the residential market is profit-driven it follows that this is a favoured provision.

The research also indicates problems for the many older people in the south and south-east of England who are self-funding. In areas where people are self-funding local authorities have far less influence on the market and, although they have the same statutory responsibilities for older people, it is notable that self-funded people receive far less assistance than those funded through the local authority. For example, an interview at a day centre with an older woman whose husband is the sole carer showed that they were finding it very difficult to obtain any form of domestic assistance from social services, compared with other interviewees who lived in sheltered housing.

Hospital procedures demonstrate a further form of unintended discrimination. On the one hand older patients are sent home too early and then have to be re-admitted. On the other hand the time taken to arrive at an assessment and package of care can be so long that the patient loses the ability to be independent, leading to another package of care and the patient remaining in the hospital bed for a long time.

It is difficult to assess whether older people with mental health problems are discriminated against because of these problems or simply because of age. Carers are necessarily the point of contact and, within this group, many of the older people aged 75 years and older are grateful for what they receive and will not complain. This has implications for both the carer and the patient and may result in a lack of communication between the medical staff and the carer, and a subsequent reduction in the level of benign care.

For further information, contact Marylynn Fyvie-Gauld, Research Officer, Health and Social Policy Research Centre, University of Brighton. Tel: 01273 643903 Email: M.M.F.Gauld @brighton.ac.uk

Referral to the right consultant and the appropriate hospital can be another area of discrimination, with some older people waiting much longer than others for similar procedures.

It has also emerged that health problems, including mental illnesses, are sometimes simply attributed to old age. Respondents have remarked that they are asked: 'What do you expect at his age?'

Clinical audits

The clinical audit programme in health organisations should present some opportunities to look at how services are meeting older people's needs and, in some cases, to compare how older people are treated in comparison with younger people. Clinical audit facilitators may be able to support clinicians in doing this. Relevant audits may usefully focus on quality issues for older people in a variety of health and social care settings. Older people should be involved in suggesting topics for audits and participating in any steering groups that support relevant audit projects.

Clinical Audit involves systematically looking at the procedures used for diagnosis, care and treatment, examining how associated resources are used and investigating the effect care has on the outcome and quality of life for the patient.

Department of Health (1998), p 22

Information from older people

The information that can be obtained from older people themselves is of fundamental importance. This may relate to their own personal experience as service users in health and social care, or may relate to experiences of friends, colleagues and families of which they have become aware in various ways. The importance of older people's evidence is borne out by a Gallup survey published by Age Concern in April 1999. This found that one in twenty people had been refused treatment at some point by the NHS. Age Concern went on to examine detailed accounts of 150 people, some of which were told by close family and friends (Age Concern England 1999). Among the harrowing stories were some from people writing on behalf of an older person, whom they felt had been 'allowed to die'. Other accounts give details of a shocking lack of dignity, poor standards of care and ageist statements from consultants and surgeons.

Further information about the use of discovery interviews and training courses can be obtained from: www.modern.nhs.uk

One of the ways in which older people's views can be obtained is through the use of discovery interviews. Discovery interviews were first used by the national Coronary Heart Disease Collaborative. They aim to elicit a detailed description of a patient's journey through the care system, pointing to gaps in services and the quality of treatment and care. The interviews are useful as they give a first-hand account from the point of view of the service user. This may well include a broad view of experiences in different parts of the health and social care system. The Collaborative now offers a two-day training programme for those wishing to make use of this tool, primarily for those working within the field of coronary heart disease.

There are many other ways of seeking information from older people, including discussions in local groups and forums. Other ways in which older people can be involved in auditing age discrimination are discussed in more detail on pp 27–35.

Information from health and social care staff

Scrutiny groups typically have some quite senior staff in attendance. It is relatively rare for clinical or care staff in junior or non-managerial posts to be involved in such groups. It is even less common for health and social care staff to have an opportunity to make their views known on where age discrimination might exist in their organisations. Direct questionnaires are one way of reaching staff (see the case study below) but, as is the case for older people themselves, this approach may not be the most successful. However, it is likely that a great deal of useful information would be provided by enabling staff to express their views in focus groups or in training and development sessions.

We ran a workshop for all sorts of staff and they all felt very enthusiastic about fighting to change systems. This inspired us to do more on training, attitudes and drilling down into what is poor practice.

Member of East Cambridgeshire and Fenland scrutiny group

Health and social care staff can be powerful advocates for those they care for. Carers and team leaders in residential care homes, supported housing workers, home care workers and community nurses are all likely to have views on whether older people get fair shares and equal treatment in relation to their needs. They may have examples of where older people have received inappropriate or inadequate care and this may inform the local audits of age discrimination. In addition, engaging staff of all levels in this work is, in itself, a means of raising awareness of age discrimination and of eventually driving forward positive change.

 Case study: Staff questionnaire in the Wirral

In the Wirral Hospital Trust the Clinical Director for the Department of Medicine for the Elderly/Rehabilitation circulated a questionnaire about age discrimination to all 5000 staff. This was sent with their salary slips at the end of September 2002. The questionnaire was designed after much discussion with many interested groups, including the NSFOP groups for Standard 1 (rooting out age discrimination) and Standard 4 (general hospital care), all of which include lay members as well as health care professionals. When the questions were agreed, they were formatted for scannable analysis. After one month, 1343 questionnaires had been returned,

i

For further information, contact Dr Debra King. Email: debra.king @whnt.nhs.uk

representing a 27 per cent response rate. As the analysis started in November 2002, it is not yet possible to give results. It will be interesting to see what kinds of issues emerge and to make a judgement on the value of this kind of approach to seeking the views of staff.

Information from voluntary organisations

Local voluntary organisations, some of which may be directly involved in the scrutiny group, can be useful partners in obtaining information about how older people fare in seeking and using health and social care services. Local Age Concern and carers' groups are obvious examples. In addition, groups that are not necessarily age-specific but which include older people within their work are also worth including. Black and minority ethnic groups, local community organisations, faith community groups and others may all have local intelligence and ways of involving older people, which are invaluable to those charged with rooting out age discrimination in health and social care.

Observation

Direct observation in health and social care organisations may provide an indication of areas and issues where a more systematic fact-finding approach would be beneficial. There are limitations to this approach because of confidentiality issues. However, some members of the scrutiny group will be in a position to report what they see in social care settings and in health care departments, clinics and wards and in the community. Also, non-executives in health organisations and local authority councillors may have direct observations that should be sought as part of the audit of age discrimination. The observations of others who regularly visit health and care organisations, such as volunteers, should also be sought.

Complaints

Most people do not complain even if they feel that they have cause to do so. Many older people are particularly reluctant to complain. Nevertheless, a number of complaints do suggest a suspicion of age discrimination on the part of the complainant. This may or may not ultimately be shown to be correct. Either way, it is helpful to monitor complaints for possible indications of age discrimination. An analysis of complaints may also be worthwhile to ensure that an assessment of trends and topics in complaints relating to older people's treatment and care is carried out. This may throw light on recurrent concerns that the complainant may not personally identify as age related, but which may sometimes appear to be so on closer examination.

Where people do not make formal complaints but express concerns that may indicate age-related issues, it will also be useful to collate this information. In the NHS, the

Patients Advice and Liaison Service (PALS) may be in a position to give anonymised information about relevant themes.

Untoward incidents

In the same way, an analysis of untoward incidents may yield information on whether there are any age-related issues that need to be addressed as a result of such incidents in health and social care settings.

Part 3
Making change happen

Part 3 looks at how to make change happen in order to root out age discrimination in health and social care. It begins by highlighting obstacles to change in this area, and identifies the need to develop strategies to address discriminatory policies or actions. It then goes on to set out some principles for making change happen. In particular, it emphasises the importance of starting with small and achievable changes and working for continuing, incremental improvements within a strategic framework for change. It also underlines the importance of being clear about priorities, and identifying and empowering people to make change happen.

7 The need to develop strategies

Change is needed to root out age discrimination. However, there are many obstacles that prevent change and this section identifies some of these.

The Department of Health NSFOP Interim Report on Age Discrimination (2002b) recognises the need to develop strategies to address both explicit and implicit policies or actions that may result in age discrimination. This section gives examples of possible strategies and emphasises the importance of building on small actions that tackle discrimination towards larger and more effective efforts.

OBSTACLES TO CHANGE

- In many health and social care organisations, tackling age discrimination is still accorded a relatively low priority, in spite of the NSFOP.
- There are too many top priorities, and age discrimination has to take its place among more urgent and more politically sensitive 'must-dos'.
- Staff and older people may themselves have ageist attitudes, of which they may or may not be aware.
- Areas of discrimination that are covered by legislation (such as race, gender and disability) may take priority within organisations.
- The scale of human and financial resources needed to tackle age discrimination may seem daunting.
- Older people are unrepresented or under-represented in the workforce of health and social care organisations.
- Constant organisational change in both health and social care organisations has distracted managerial attention away from developmental issues such as tackling age discrimination.
- Monitoring change can be difficult, especially where age discrimination is subtle or hidden.

Figure 3 *below* illustrates NSFOP guidance on developing strategies to tackle discriminatory policies.

3 | **DEVELOPING STRATEGIES TO ADDRESS EXPLICIT AND IMPLICIT POLICIES AND ACTION**

Explicit policies / actions

that locally there is as full a picture as possible of the current policy and practice

that this is reviewed and looked at critically

action is taken to correct / remove any discriminatory criteria

the development of a system of monitoring, benchmarking and continuing review of access to treatments / services, feedback and evaluation

Implicit policies / actions / decision-making

Raise awareness of the issue of age discrimination

Ensure the issue is covered in personal and professional development and training programmes for current staff

Ensure the issue is covered in training and educational courses

Link to the development of monitoring, benchmarking and continued review, feedback and evaluation

Source: Department of Health 2002b, p 16

Most scrutiny groups have been preoccupied in their early stages with the challenge of identifying age discrimination and finding appropriate methods to do so. The next challenge is deciding what to do with the information that is gathered on age discrimination in order to translate knowledge into action and positive change. This often seems very daunting, as some changes may require a major investment or realignment of resources in order to secure improvements, while other aspects of change rely more on changing people's attitudes. Although it is not possible to consider everything at once or to address all instances of age discrimination at the same time, it is very important to make a start and to build on small actions towards larger and more effective efforts to root out age discrimination.

> *Auditing age discrimination is very much a hearts and minds issue. We need to have both stick and carrots, but it is not obvious what the carrots are. We need to grow our own carrots and see the benefits for ourselves.*
>
> Member of Leeds scrutiny group
>
> *The main task is to get people to sign up to the framework and make robust links with older people's leads and champion the process.*
>
> Member of Leeds scrutiny group

8 Principles for making change happen

There are a number of key principles that help to make change happen in this area. This section sets out these principles and emphasises the importance of starting with small and achievable change, and working for continuing, incremental improvements within a strategic framework for change.

Experience to date has suggested a number of principles that assist in making change in this area. These are considered below:

TACKLING AGE DISCRIMINATION: PRINCIPLES FOR MAKING CHANGE HAPPEN

- Be explicit about priorities for change.
- Make clear recommendations for change.
- Identify areas where small changes can be made now, as part of a longer-term strategy.
- Build on sustainable, incremental improvements.
- Plan training and development that links awareness of age discrimination with action planning for change.
- Link action to other relevant initiatives for change.
- Ensure that there are structures to link the scrutiny panel with Boards/Councils for resourcing and implementation of change.
- Involve and empower staff to make changes.
- Identify key people who can take action and be allies in making change happen.
- Be clear that tackling age discrimination is an ongoing process, not a one-off event.
- Learn from the experience of others.

 Be explicit about priorities for change

It is easy to be daunted by the size of the agenda for change. A feeling of helplessness can ensue in the absence of prioritisation. It is helpful to be explicit about the criteria on which prioritisation is based. These may include a variety of factors, such as:

- the impact on older people's lives
- the concerns of older people
- the feasibility of making a difference quickly
- opportunities to access specific funding (for example for converting mixed-sex wards to single-sex wards)
- opportunities for partnership work across health and social care organisations.

Older people and health and social care staff should be involved in determining the criteria for prioritising action.

 ## Make clear recommendations for change

It is essential to be clear about where and how change is necessary. Recommendations should be clear and as specific as possible. Generalisations about ageism are unlikely to lead directly to change, while specific illustrations of age discrimination (for example in staffing levels, skill mix, poor environments for care) are more readily translated into planned change.

 ## Identify areas where small changes can be made now, as part of a longer-term strategy

A long-term strategy for rooting out age discrimination is an important part of planning for change, since some of the necessary changes may require major investment or realignment of resources, or different ways of working in partnership with older people. However, the key to rooting out age discrimination is to identify areas where small changes can be made, in line with the overall strategic aims, without undue delay. Since ageist practices often reflect outmoded attitudes and practices, a great deal can be done by starting with small and achievable changes in how older people are cared for in health and social care.

For example, in Hillingdon Hospital it was decided to consider how the issue of feeding older people could be addressed. It was decided that work would start on the two wards for older people and extend to the whole hospital later. The work could be done in conjunction with ward staff and the wider aim was to work together to improve the catering services for older people in hospital.

 ## Build on sustainable, incremental improvements

Once change is underway, no matter how small, it is important to review it in order to identify opportunities for building on successful change. For example, changes made in one day centre may be easily rolled out to others. Improvements in arrangements to ensure dignity for older people on one ward may serve as a model for others to follow.

 ## Plan training and development that links awareness of age discrimination with action planning for change

It is possible to drive forward short-term change by managerial edict, but sustainable change requires an understanding and awareness throughout the organisation about what change is required and why. Without a shared understanding, even apparently robust plans for change can flounder under the weight of inertia or outright opposition. Awareness and understanding of age discrimination must be linked to an action planning process that clearly sets out a route map for change. This will need to identify lead people to drive forward change and to be accountable for progress against agreed goals and timetables.

Training alone cannot bring about change. It must be linked to ways of making change happen. Different groups of staff and older people will be able to contribute to the process of change in different ways. Training and development sessions provide an opportunity to identify some of those ways.

 ## Link action to other relevant initiatives for change

Planning to change age-discriminatory practice should be linked to other related initiatives. It is important to link into these, wherever possible, to achieve synergy. For example, work on *Essence of Care*, the Department of Health's patient-focused benchmarking for health care practitioners (Department of Health 2001c), is integral to many of the issues that will need to be addressed as part of rooting out age discrimination. Another example of a relevant initiative is the introduction of the single assessment process and the emphasis on meeting the needs of individuals as part of Standard 2 of the NSFOP on person-centred care.

In a climate where there are so many targets that must be met and policies that must be implemented, it is extremely important to identify levers for change and to make common ground, wherever possible, on related targets and initiatives. In fact, a number of important initiatives fit together very well. For example, modernising health and social care can only happen when the independence of older people is promoted. This is closely linked with involving older people in a whole range of ways and with looking closely at services to ensure that older people are not marginalised or treated unfairly by the way in which they are organised or delivered.

 ## Ensure that there are structures to link the scrutiny group with Boards/Councils for resourcing and implementation of change

Early experiences of some scrutiny groups suggest that they are not always clear about how to move from the collection of information towards ensuring that Boards and Councils plan change as a result of this information. The NSFOP stipulates that there should be an elected council member or an NHS non-executive director who will lead for older people across each organisation. As well as being responsible for ensuring that older people become and remain a priority within their organisation and supporting implementation of the NSF, they are responsible for presenting a progress report to their Board (NHS) or the scrutiny committee responsible for social services every six months. At present, this is probably not happening everywhere. Even when it does happen, it is questionable whether a formal report to a committee or Board, as part of an overcrowded agenda, will hit the spot. In addition, age-discrimination scrutiny groups should also give thought to developing more robust ways to plan and progress executive action to deliver change to an agreed action plan. Where necessary, this will include getting concerns translated into material for business or annual plans and costed developments.

 ## Involve and empower staff to make changes

Staff in health and social care organisations, and particularly those in basic grade posts, often feel as powerless as older people themselves in bringing about change. Yet staff, like older people, are extremely important in their potential to make change happen. They may also stand in the way of change or slow it down if they feel that it is inappropriate or unachievable. All too often, a vision for change develops in the minds of managers and is not adequately rooted in or shared with other staff. This problem does not require elaborate solutions. Opportunities for communicating with staff at an individual or team level already exist. Individual supervision sessions, team meetings, departmental briefings and many other ways can be used to inform and involve staff. It is also helpful to engage staff in identifying which sections of the workforce can be most influential in making different kinds of change happen. Some aspects will be common to all, while others will be best addressed either by commissioners or providers of services.

Identify key people who can take action and be allies in making change happen

In one sense, making change happen is always a process of skilful negotiation, in which it is helpful to identify potential allies and keep them informed on how and where they can support change. Non-executive champions in health organisations or councillors in local authorities, as well as clinical champions, are the most obvious allies. However, other colleagues may need to be primed to see where they can impact on age discrimination. For example, directors of human resources may be helpful in taking forward the training and development aspects of the change process, and directors of finance need to be committed to negotiating effectively in the three-year local delivery plans where there are revenue or capital implications in addressing age discrimination.

Be clear that tackling age discrimination is an ongoing process, not a one-off event

The Department of Health recognises that rooting out age discrimination is a long-term goal. Although certain milestones have already been passed, it is acknowledged that year-on-year progress will be required. Indeed, if the experience of addressing other forms of discrimination has any predictive value, it may be wise to see the process of rooting out age discrimination as an ongoing one. At a local level, the challenge is to find ways of keeping the bigger picture in mind, while working now for immediate improvements. Achieving recognisable change can energise people to continue with the work. It is important to do this as keeping the momentum going is a real challenge.

Learn from the experience of others

See:
www.doh.gov.uk/nsf/
olderpeople.htm

As all health and social care organisations are facing similar challenges in identifying age discrimination and taking action to eliminate it, it is important to learn from the experiences of others. Equally, it is important to let others know how you have approached the audit of age discrimination, what difficulties you have faced and potential solutions to those difficulties. In addition to local forums for sharing information and experience, the discussion forum and notice board of the Older People's Champions may be useful.

References

Age Concern and British Geriatrics Society (2002). *Implementation of the National Service Framework and Intermediate Care seen from the Geriatricians' and Older People's Perspectives: A joint statement from Age Concern and the British Geriatrics Society.*

Age Concern England (1999). *Turning Your Back on Us: Older people and the NHS.* London: Age Concern England.

Age Concern Scotland (1994). *New Ways of Working. Fife User Panel's First Annual Report.* Kircaldy: Age Concern Scotland.

Age Concern Wandsworth (2000). *Older People and Alcohol Misuse: Setting the agenda. Report of a one-day conference organised by Age Concern Wandsworth.*

Barker J, Bullen M and de Ville J (1999). *Reference Manual for Public Involvement.* London: Lambeth, Southwark and Lewisham Health Authority.

Barnes M and Bennett G (1998). Frail bodies, courageous voices: older people influencing community care. *Health and Social Care in the Community* 6 (2): 102–111.

Cabinet Office (1999a). *Involving Users: Improving the delivery of local public services: a report from the National Consumer Council, Consumer Congress and the Service First Unit in the Cabinet Office.* London: Cabinet Office 1999.

Cabinet Office (1999b). *Involving Users: Improving the delivery of healthcare: a report from the National Consumer Council, Consumer Congress and the Service First Unit in the Cabinet Office.* London: Cabinet Office 1999.

Department of Health (1998). *A First Class Service: Quality in the new NHS.* London: Department of Health.

Department of Health (2001a). *National Service Framework for Older People.* London: Department of Health.

Department of Health (2001b). *National Service Framework for Older People. Audit of policies for age-related criteria: A guide.* London: Department of Health.

Department of Health (2001c). *The Essence of Care: Patient focused benchmarking for health care practitioners.* London: Department of Health.

Department of Health (2002a). *Fair Access to Care Services: Guidance on eligibility criteria for adult social care.* London: Department of Health.

Department of Health (2002b). *National Service Framework for Older People: Interim report on age discrimination.* London: Department of Health.

Department of Health (2002c). *Information Strategy for Older People in England.* London: Department of Health.

Department of Health (2002d). *Developing Services for Minority Ethnic Older People: The audit tool. Practice guidance for councils with social services responsibilities, in support of From Lip Service to Real Service.* London: Department of Health.

Department of Health (2002e). *Fair Access to Care Services: Guidance on eligibility criteria for adult social care.* Local Authority Circular LAC(2002)13. London: Department of Health.

Department of Trade and Industry (2002). *Equality and Diversity: Making it happen*. London: Department of Trade and Industry.

Dunning A (2000). *Dignity on the Ward: Advocacy with older people in hospital*. London: Help the Aged.

Ellis J, Harding T and Owen T (2003). *Involving Older People in the New NHS: A guide*. London: Help the Aged.

European Council (2000). *Employment Directive on Equal Treatment*. European Council Directive 2000/78/EC.

Hanratty B, Lawlor D, Robinson M, Sapsford R, Greenwood D and Hall A (2000). Sex differences in risk factors, treatment and mortality after acute myocardial infarction – an observational study. *Journal of Epidemiology and Community Health*, 54 (12) 912–916.

Health Advisory Service (1998). *Not Because They are Old*. Brighton: Pavilion Publishing.

Help the Aged, Orders of St John and the University of Sheffield School of Nursing and Midwifery (1999a). *Dignity on the Ward: Promoting excellence in care: Good practice in acute hospital care for older people*. London: Help the Aged.

Help the Aged (1999b). *Dignity on the Ward: Promoting excellence in care. Good practice in acute hospital care for older people. A summary and checklist designed for community health councils, voluntary groups and campaigners*. London: Help the Aged.

Help the Aged (2000). *Our Future Health: Older people's priorities for health and social care. A report by the Health and Older People Group (HOPe)*. London: Help the Aged.

Help the Aged (2001). *Dignity on the Ward: Towards dignity. A report from Policy Research on Ageing and Ethnicity (PRIAE) for Help the Aged Dignity on the Ward Campaign*. London: Help the Aged.

Help the Aged (2002a). *Age Discrimination in Public Policy: A review of the evidence*. London: Help the Aged.

Help the Aged (2002b). *The Voice of Older People: An introduction to senior citizens' forums*. London: Help the Aged.

Herklots H (2002). *Getting Involved: Working with older people*. 6(1) p 28–31. London: Pavilion.

London Borough of Tower Hamlets (2001). *Audit of Age-related Policies and Practices, October 2001*. Committee Paper. London: London Borough of Tower Hamlets.

Office of National Statistics (2000). *Life Expectancy at Birth (Years) by Health and Local Authorities in the United Kingdom 1998–2000*. London: ONS.

Office of National Statistics (2002). *Health Statistics Quarterly 14*, Summer 2002, p 21. London: ONS.

Roberts E (2000). *Age Discrimination in Health and Social Care: A briefing note*. London: King's Fund (available at www.kingsfund.org.uk).

Roberts E, Robinson J and Seymour L (2002). *Old Habits Die Hard: Tackling age discrimination in health and social care*. London: King's Fund.

Robinson J (2002). *Age Equality in Health and Social Care: A paper presented to IPPR seminar, 28 January 2002*. London: King's Fund (available at www.kingsfund.org.uk).

Useful websites

Age Concern
www.ace.org.uk

Better Government for Older People
www.bettergovernmentforolderpeople.gov.uk

Department of Health: National Service Framework for Older People
www.doh.gov.uk/nsf/olderpeople.htm

Department of Health: _Toolkit for Older People's Champions_
Available at www.doh.gov.uk/nsf/olderpeople.htm

Department of Trade and Industry website on tackling age discrimination and promoting age diversity in employment
www.agepositive.gov.uk

Help the Aged
www.helptheaged.org.uk

King's Fund
www.kingsfund.org.uk

NHS Modernisation Agency
www.modern.nhs.uk

Index

Related King's Fund titles

Great to be Grey
HOW CAN THE NHS RECRUIT AND RETAIN MORE OLDER STAFF?
Sandra Meadows

This research paper looks at how early retirement is affecting the NHS, and why it is happening. It asks what the NHS can learn from other sectors about recruiting and retaining older people. It is invaluable reading for HR directors and management staff in the NHS, policy-makers in national and local government, workforce development confederations and organisations concerned with workforce issues and older people.

ISBN 1 85717 471 2   December 2002   44pp   Price: £8.00

Managing the Pressure
EMERGENCY HOSPITAL ADMISSIONS IN LONDON 1997–2001
Michael Damiani and Jennifer Dixon

This report examines the nature of emergency admissions in London, pointing out that the main peaks in demand appear to be due to respiratory disease during the Christmas period. Chronic disease in the elderly is a major factor, and residents of the East End of London seem to be affected more than average. All these peaks happen at the same time every year and are therefore highly predictable. Improved management of these patients might alleviate pressures on hospitals during busy periods, and a number of methods by which this can be achieved are proposed.

ISBN 1 85717 461 5   January 2002   30pp   Price: £5.99

Old Habits Die Hard
Emilie Roberts, Janice Robinson, Linda Seymour

This report shows that managers in NHS and social care organisations struggle to prevent discrimination on the grounds of age. Based on a telephone survey of 75 senior managers in hospitals, primary care groups, community trusts and social services departments, it shows that while the majority support moves to combat age discrimination, they lack practical tools for the job.

ISBN 1 85717 462 3   January 2002   50pp   Price: £6.99

Paying for Old Age
INTERIM RESEARCH REPORT FROM THE KING'S FUND LONG-TERM FINANCING PROJECT
Chris Deeming & Justin Keen

The Government is asking the public to take more responsibility for their own long-term care, but at the same time, it is also asking people to contribute more to their pensions. Is this sustainable? *Paying for Old Age* shows that people in their fifties – tomorrow's pensioners – will find it difficult to save money to pay for their long-term care needs, and will be no better off than today's pensioners.

ISBN 1 85717 404 6   October 2000   20pp   Price: £3.00

Primary Care Groups and Older People
SIGNS OF PROGRESS
Margaret Edwards and Emilie Roberts

A study of how primary care groups (PCGs) are working with partner organisations and older people in their localities. Based on the progress made by five PCGs towards improving services for older people and their carers, this report highlights the factors that influence success in this area and the implications for policy and practice.

ISBN 1 85717 434 8   November 2000   55pp   Price: £6.99

Towards a New Social Compact for Care in Old Age
Janice Robinson (ed)

The Government is planning controversial changes to the funding of long term care for older people. This important book explores the past and future of policy in this area and reflects the changing balance between the state's and the individual's responsibilities to cover risks associated with ill health and disabilities. Is current policy understood and supported by the public? Should the Government restate and perhaps reform the social compact that exists between the public and the Government?

ISBN 1 85717 444 5   July 2001   80pp   Price: £8.99

 # Order form

Title	ISBN	Price	Quantity
Great to be Grey	1 85717 471 2	£8.00	
Managing the Pressure	1 85717 461 5	£5.99	
Old Habits Die Hard	1 85717 462 3	£6.99	
Paying for Old Age	1 85717 404 6	£3.00	
Primary Care Groups and Older People	1 85717 434 8	£6.99	
Towards a New Social Compact for Care in Old Age	1 85717 444 5	£8.99	

Total £ for titles

Postage and packing

Total order £

☐ I enclose a cheque for £_____ made payable to King's Fund

☐ Please charge £_____ to my credit card account (Please circle: Mastercard/Visa/Visa Delta/Switch)

Card No: _____

Expiry Date: _____

Issue No/Valid from date: _____

Title (Dr, Mr, Ms, Mrs, Miss): _____

First name: _____

Surname: _____

Job title: _____

Organisation: _____

Address: _____

_____

_____ Postcode: _____

Tel: _____ Fax:_____

E-mail: _____

Billing address (if different):

_____

_____

_____ Postcode: _____

POSTAGE AND PACKING – Please add **10%** of the total order value for **UK** (up to a maximum fee of £8.00). Please add **20%** if ordering from **Europe** (up to a maximum of £15.00). Please add **30%** if ordering from the **rest of the world** (up to a maximum of £30.00).

PLEASE NOTE – Shortages must be reported within ten days of delivery date. **We can invoice for orders of £35.00 and over** if a purchase order is supplied.

Please detach and send this order form to
KING'S FUND
11–13 CAVENDISH SQUARE, LONDON W1G 0AN
TEL **020 7307 2591**   FAX **020 7307 2801**
www.kingsfundbookshop.org.uk